Financing Health Care for the Poor

Published in cooperation with The Urban Institute, Washington, D.C.

Financing Health Care for the Poor

The Medicaid Experience

John Holahan
The Urban Institute

Lexington Books
D.C. Heath and Company
Lexington, Massachusetts
Toronto   London

Library of Congress Cataloging in Publication Data

Holahan, John F.
   Financing health care for the poor.

   Bibliography: p.
   1. Medicaid. 2. Poor—Medical care—United States. I. Title. [DNLM:
1. Medicaid. W275 AA1 H72f]
HD7102.U4H58   368.4'2'00973   74-26756
ISBN 0-669-97634-2

Published simultaneously in Canada.

Printed in the United States of America.

International Standard Book Number: 0-669-97634-2

Library of Congress Catalog Card Number: 74-26756

Contents

List of Tables   vii

Acknowledgments   ix

Chapter 1   Introduction   1

Chapter 2   **Equity, Efficiency, and Rising Costs**   9

Equity   11
Efficiency   23
The Growth in the Cost of Medicaid   27

Chapter 3   **Hospital Inpatient Care**   33

Introduction   33
Hypotheses   37
Data   42
Results   44
Summary   49

Chapter 4   **Physician Services**   51

Introduction   51
Hypotheses   56
Results   61
Summary   70

Chapter 5   **Alternatives to Medicaid**   73

Changing the Structure of Medicaid   73
Four Alternative Plans   77
Coverage of Long-Term Care in National
     Health Insurance   92
Summary   93

Chapter 6   **Increasing the Efficiency of the System**   97

Hospital Reimbursement   98
Physician Reimbursement   100
Area-wide Health Planning   102
Utilization Review   104
Health Maintenance Organizations and
   Medical Society Foundations   105
Conclusions   108

Chapter 7   **Summary and Conclusions**   109

Lessons of Medicaid   109
Prospects for Reform   115
Concluding Remarks   119

                    Appendixes   121

Appendix A   Data Sources   123

Appendix B   Users Per Eligible and Expenditures per
                       User for Selected Services for All
                       States   131

Appendix C   Means and Standard Deviations of Variables
                       in Regression Analysis   141

Appendix D   Data Sources for Time Series Analysis   143

                    Bibliography   147

                    About the Author   153

List of Tables

2-1   Total Medicaid Expenditures by Type of
        Service and Eligibility Category, 1970   10

2-2   Maximum Annual Cash Assistance Payments
        for Four-Person Families, 1971, by State   14

2-3   Variations in Medicaid Coverage of the
        Poor, 1970   16

2-4   Provision of Optional Services Under
        Medicaid, 1972   19

2-5   Variations in Medicaid Expenditures Per
        Eligible, 1970 Cash Assistance
        Recipients   22

2-6   The Growth of Medicaid Costs, 1967-1972   29

3-1   Hospital Inpatient Care, Expenditures
        Per Eligible, by State, 1970   34

3-2   Methods of Physician Reimbursement,
        by State   40

3-3   Hospital Inpatient Care Regression
        Results   45

3-4   Selected Elasticity Estimates, Hospital
        Inpatient Care   46

4-1   Physician and Hospital Outpatient Services,
        Expenditures Per Eligible, by State, 1970   52

4-2   Physician Services Regression Results   62

4-3   Hospital Outpatient Services Regression   64
        Results

4-4   Selected Elasticity Estimates, Medical
        and Hospital Outpatient Services   65

4-5   Price Differentials Under Alternative
        Reimbursement Arrangements, Assuming
        No Supply Effects   66

5-1   Premiums and Cost Sharing in the
        Administration's Assisted Health
        Insurance Plan   79

5-2   Medical Care Outlays for Three
        Hypothetical Families   80

5-3   Medical Care Outlays (Including Premiums)
        Paid by Four-Person Family Under CHIP
        Plan   81

5-4   Medical Care Outlays (Including
        Contributions) Paid by Four-Person
        Family Under Kennedy-Mills Plan   88

Acknowledgments

I would like to express my appreciation and gratitude for the valuable contributions of several individuals. First, William Pollak, Jeffrey Koshel, Jerry Turem, Uwe Reinhardt, and Karen Davis provided many helpful insights and suggestions at various stages in the preparation of the book. Second, Lydia Skloven, Patricia Barry, and Joanne Hilferty contributed valuable research assistance throughout the study. Finally, I am indebted to Ann Best, Brenda Chapman, and Melissa Penney for excellent secretarial assistance. Any shortcomings, errors, and omissions are solely the responsibility of the author.

I am also extremely grateful for the financial support given by the Department of Health, Education and Welfare and the Ford Foundation. The research described in Chapters 2 through 4 were financed through HEW contract number HEW-74-113 and grant number 18-P-5665/3-01. The work presented in Chapters 5 and 6 was financed by the Ford Foundation.

Financing Health Care for the Poor

1 Introduction

The Medicaid program was created as part of the 1965 amendments to the Social Security Act, which greatly expanded the role of the federal government in health care financing. Title XVIII established the nationwide hospital and medical insurance program for elderly Social Security recipients known as Medicare. Title XIV established the medical assistance program known as Medicaid as part of the federal-state public assistance system. The program has grown considerably since its adoption and currently finances health care services for over twenty million individuals. Costs have risen at rapid rates and, unlike Medicare, it has been a very controversial and unpopular program. One of the most powerful arguments for a national health insurance program is the need for reform of Medicaid and the rest of the system of care for the poor.

This book is the result of an effort to see what might be learned from the program that would be useful in the design of its successor. We have examined equity and efficiency issues in the structure of the program and have analyzed the growth in costs from 1967 to 1972. We have empirically investigated the effects of alternative reimbursement arrangements and the geographical distribution of hospital beds and physicians as well as factors such as income, education, and race on service utilization within the program. We also provide an analysis of the impact four national health insurance plans, proposed in part as alternatives to Medicaid, would have on the financing of services for the poor. Finally, we consider alternative approaches to increasing the efficiency of the delivery system so that reform of the health financing system for the poor can be implemented without serious adverse effects on prices of various services.

The Medicaid program today is a result of an increasing involvement on the part of the federal government in the financing of health care services for the poor. The provision of some form of medical assistance to the poor had long been a part of the welfare system in many states. Prior to 1935 this assistance was available to the poor through publicly financed hospitals and clinics based on state and local decisions, but no federal standards existed on a national basis. The Social Security Act of 1936 provided for federal matching only on payments for medical care expenses made directly to welfare recipients. It excluded direct payment to hospitals, physicians, or clinics. Payments to recipients for maintenance and medical assistance were subject to federal and state matching maximums per month per recipient. Participation in the federal categorical programs was optional for the states and, in general, the provision of medical services to the poor remained a minor part of welfare assistance until the

1

1950

passage of a federally supported program of direct medical vendor payments in 1950.

The 1950 amendments to the Social Security Act provided for federal matching funds to the states for payment of medical services directly to physicians, hospitals, and others who provided medical care to those persons on public assistance. In the years following the 1950 amendments several changes were made in the federal matching formulae to encourage state participation. By 1960 four-fifths of the states had federally approved plans for making vendor payments under all public assistance programs at a cost of $514 million annually.

The passage of the Kerr-Mills Act of 1960 marked a significant increase in the level of federal concern with the delivery of medical services to the poor. The bill provided higher levels of federal matching grants under Old Age Assistance and, for the first time, applied to open ended total expenditures rather than to individual payment maximums or the averaging of individual recipients' payments. Of more importance was the creation of a new category of assistance which was termed "medically needy." A separate program of federal grants for Medical Assistance for the Aged (MAA) was established. This program was the first designed to provide benefits to persons who were not financially eligible for public assistance but who needed cash assistance to cover the cost of medical care. State participation was optional and each state set its own standard of medical and financial need. By the end of 1965 all fifty states and four jurisdictions had federally approved vendor payment programs for medical care and forty-seven states had approved plans for MAA. Total medical vendor payments had risen to $1.3 billion per year.

Medicaid was established in 1965 and was adopted by over half the states the following year. The most important features of the program were the following:

1. It consolidated the program of medical assistance replacing the vendor payments under the categorical assistance and Medical Assistance for the Aged programs, with the stipulation that by 1970 federal payments for medical care would only be made under Medicaid.
2. It increased the rate of federal financial participation in the costs of medical care.
3. It required each state to cover all persons eligible for cash assistance.
4. It permitted states to include the medically needy aged, blind, disabled, and families at the option of the state (with federal cost sharing).
5. It required all participating states to include inpatient and outpatient hospital services, other laboratory and X-ray services, skilled nursing home services, and physician services and permitted many other services at the option of the states.

The immediate objective of Medicaid was to encourage states to establish a unified single medical assistance program. The program was also to include coverage of common levels of medical care, for at least all recipients of federally-subsidized cash assistance. States were allowed to define their own standard of who was medically needy. The act encouraged liberalization of eligibility standards and the provision of comprehensive medical services for all persons included under a state's definition of "medically needy."

The act did not require the states to develop such a program, but considerable pressure was placed on them to do so by providing that after December 31, 1969 there would be no further federal funds for medical vendor payments under the categorical titles for OAA, AFDC, AB, APTD, and Kerr-Mills.[a] By the end of 1966, twenty-six states were participating in the program. By 1970, only Alaska and Arizona did not have Medicaid programs in operation, claiming inordinately high costs would result because nearly all Eskimos and Indians would be eligible. As this is written, only Arizona does not have a program.

Criticism of the program began shortly after implementation, mainly because of the cost of its operation. The federal share was greatly underestimated and individual states were confronted with reducing services to reduce costs, which threatened to overrun total state budgets for cash assistance. It was originally anticipated that Medicaid would add only $250 million to vendor payments of $1.3 billion in 1965. Instead, total program costs mushroomed to $3.2 billion in 1968, $4.8 billion in 1970, and $8.0 billion in 1972. It now seems clear that there was little consideration given to the number potentially eligible or to the demand for services provided free of any user charge. There was little understanding of the capacity of the delivery system to respond to a major shift in demand, nor of the adverse incentive effects of various methods used to pay for services.

Implied in the legislation was the notion that Medicaid would provide financial access to a basic level of medical care for all in need. Yet states were allowed to individually determine eligibility standards and benefit packages. The result has been that some states provide coverage for most of the poor and many of the near-poor, while others cover only a small proportion of the poor. In addition, some states provide only those services required by the federal guidelines, and still others provide a comprehensive range of services beyond federal requirements. A program that is federally sponsored but participated in at the option of the states and administered locally has been unable to solve the problem of providing access to medical care for all those in need.

The 1967 amendments to the Social Security Act reflected the increased concern of federal, state, and local governments with the administration of Medicaid. These amendments centered mainly on greater control and supervision of local programs in the areas of controlling costs and ensuring quality of care in a program supported in large part by federal funds. Federal guidelines were

[a]OAA   – Old Age Assistance
  AFDC – Aid to Families with Dependent Children
  AB   – Aid to the Blind
  APTD – Aid to the Permanently and Totally Disabled

instituted which required states to review on a continual basis the costs, administration, utilization, and quality of medical care being provided under local Medicaid programs. Periodic reviews were required to appraise the utilization and quality of care in long-term institutions. To further insure that long-term care in nursing homes was adequate, federal standards for nursing homes were established.

The 1969 amendments again reflected a continuing concern over the rising costs of Medicaid to the federal and state governments. The 1975 target date requiring all states to provide a program of comprehensive care was postponed until 1977. The states were also allowed to drop optional services when necessitated by state budget pressures.

The 1972 amendments to the Social Security Act (P.L. 92-603) made many important changes in the program. It eliminated the requirement that states move toward comprehensive Medicaid programs. States were also required to use enrollment fees, graduated by income, for the medically indigent. In addition, they were permitted to employ nominal deductibles and co-payments on all services used by the medically indigent and on optional services used by cash assistance recipients. Other measures were taken to directly control costs. First, the amendments permitted HEW to withhold or reduce reimbursement amounts to providers for depreciation, interest and, for proprietary institutions, return on equity, which are related to capital expenditures not consistent with state or local health plans. Second, they provided for reductions in the federal matching assistance percentage for states which fail to establish effective utilization review programs. Third, they provide for establishment of independent Professional Standards Review Organizations (PSROs) formed by organizations which are representative of practicing physicians in local areas. PSROs would assume responsibility for comprehensive review to determine whether services are "(1) medically necessary and (2) provided in accordance with professional standards."[1]

Despite the program restructuring reflected in these amendments, interest in the reform or replacement of Medicaid remains strong. Most national health insurance plans call for elimination of the program. For example, the proposals introduced by Senators Kennedy and Javits provide for a single comprehensive program covering the entire population. Medicaid would also cease to exist under the Long-Ribicoff plan and the most recent Nixon Administration proposal. In this book, we examine several issues raised by the program which we believe are relevant to the consideration of national health insurance legislation.

Chapter 2 contains an investigation of equity and efficiency issues in Medicaid and an analysis of the growth in Medicaid costs over time. An effort is made to show how state administration of the program has resulted in large differentials in eligibility criteria and benefit provision. We show the impact of these differences on the coverage of those individuals considered poor under the

Census definition of poverty. In addition, estimates of the variation in the value of the Medicaid program to eligibles in different states are provided. We then discuss the lack of efficiency inducing incentives in the program, focusing in particular on the methods of reimbursing hospitals and physicians. Finally, the growth in Medicaid costs from 1967 to 1972 is analyzed. There is an apparent concern that the program is out of control, that costs have escalated for reasons that defy understanding. We consider the increase in expenditures for three groups: the aged (OAA), the disabled (APTD), and families with dependent children (AFDC). We show that, for most eligibility categories, the primary reason for increases in Medicaid costs over time has been the increases in the number of people eligible. During this period new states have entered the program and public assistance eligibility criteria were greatly liberalized, increasing the number of persons receiving public assistance and thereby becoming eligible for Medicaid. The participation rate, the percentage of eligibles using services, and prices have risen, but not nearly as fast as the number of eligibles. Services per user, in most groups, were either constant or falling.

In Chapters 3 and 4, we present an extensive empirical investigation of use of health care services under the program. We examine the use of selected "mandatory" services (hospital inpatient care, medical services, and hospital outpatient services) by three cash assistance groups in both 1969 and 1970. The variance across states in both utilization rates and in such factors as methods of paying for physician services, the supply of hospital beds and physicians, income, etc., permits an analysis of several policy issues relevant to the efficient financing and delivery of care to the poor. Such issues include the effects of different reimbursement arrangements, the maldistribution of medical resources, income, rural residence, etc., on use of services by the poor.

The effect of the supply and distribution of health care resources on utilization is of great concern to policymakers. For example, it is often argued that the growth of hospital beds has led directly to increases in the demand for hospital inpatient services rather than through a fall in price. Does this argument hold for the Medicaid population, and if so, can Medicaid costs be affected by efforts to limit the supply of beds? It is also argued that because of supply constraints, eliminating the monetary barrier to use of ambulatory services for Medicaid eligibles is not sufficient to insure appropriate utilization of services. At the same time, there is concern that an abundant supply of physicians will affect the demand for physician services not only by reducing delays or inconvenience, but also by directly affecting the demand for services. It is alleged that some of the physician-induced demand for services is unnecessary and reflects an inefficient and costly use of resources. Is there evidence that supply factors affect the demand for ambulatory services in the Medicaid program either by reducing delays or inconvenience or by directly affecting the demand for services? Does the availability of physicians result in a substitution of outpatient for inpatient care? Does the relative availability of surgeons influence the use of hospital beds and the overall use of physician services in the Medicaid program? In general, we found no evidence that hospital bed supply affects use of hospital services under Medicaid. However, we did find evidence that physician availability influences the use of ambulatory services and that an increase in the outlays for inpatient care occurs when physicians are in relative abundance.

The impact of different reimbursement arrangements is another important policy issue. Under Medicaid several states reimburse physicians on the basis of "reasonable charges," which gives physicians considerable control over prices. On the other hand, some states have instituted fee schedules to control physician fees. Very little is known about the impact of alternative reimbursement schemes on utilization and Medicaid costs. Do fee schedules reduce average costs significantly? Do physicians respond by prescribing greater amounts of discretionary services or do they respond by not participating as heavily in the program? Are there differences in the utilization of services (in physical units) that are attributable to different methods of reimbursement? Do restrictive reimbursement arrangements induce a substitution of hospital outpatient care for physician services? In general, we found that fee schedules had remarkably large effects on per user expenditures for both hospital and medical services. We found no evidence that reimbursement arrangements cause a substitution of hospital outpatient care for physician services.

There is also interest among policymakers in the effect of income on the use of health services by the poor. Most studies of the impact of income have concluded that it has little effect on utilization. But such findings are typically generated by studies of the general population. The impact of variations in income at the low end of the distribution are largely unknown. If income elasticities are large at the bottom of the income distribution, reform of income security programs may have unexpected effects on the use of health services. Our results indicated that the use of physician services by Medicaid eligibles is quite responsive to income.

Finally, there is concern over utilization differences between urban and rural residents and between whites and non-whites. Do Medicaid eligibles living in urban areas use more services, when income, race and other factors are considered, than eligibles living in rural areas? Are there differences between blacks and whites in the utilization of services under Medicaid that cannot be attributed to income, education, place of residence, etc.? Or has complete financial coverage of basic services been sufficient to eliminate the barriers of race and distance? We found clear evidence of greater use of ambulatory services by urban residents as well as evidence of less use of all services by non-whites.

In Chapter 5, we consider criteria for an equitable and efficient program for financing health care services for the poor and show that the present Medicaid program does not meet these criteria. We examine the effects four proposed national health insurance programs would have on low income families and individuals. Cost sharing provisions, reimbursement arrangements, administration and financing mechanisms are considered. Any reform of Medicaid which would expand coverage would increase the need for methods of improving the efficiency of the system. In Chapter 6, we describe several existing approaches and discuss issues involved in each, drawing on published literature and our own research.

This study has not been an effort to provide a pervasive examination of all the health care problems of low income people. The focus is rather on issues in the financing of health services for the poor. Among the many issues not addressed in this book, two stand out in importance. First, while a large share of Medicaid outlays finance long-term care, we are concerned almost exclusively with acute care. Financing and organization of long-term care involves issues which are unlike those for acute care and which must necessarily be addressed in their own right. Second, the objective of a program which finances health care for the poor should be improvements in health status, not merely health services utilization. To the extent increased utilization by the poor improves health, that objective is being met. But concern with utilization can obscure the importance of other factors such as nutrition, air and water pollution, and housing decay which also affect health. A rational strategy for improving the health of the poor would necessarily involve the difficult assessment of the relative costs and benefits of improvements in diet, environmental protection, etc., and increased use of health services.

Note

1. For a comprehensive summary of the provisions of the 1972 Social Security Amendments as they affect Medicaid, see U.S. Department of Health, Education, and Welfare, National Center for Social Statistics, *Medicaid*, 3, 1 (Nov. 1972).

2

Equity, Efficiency, and Rising Costs

The benefits from the Medicaid Program are often overlooked amidst the nearly constant barrage of criticism. Medicaid has provided financial coverage of medical services for over eighteen million persons per year (1972). It has caused an increase in the number of providers willing to care for the poor in most parts of the country. Medicaid pays for premiums ($147.6 million in fiscal year 1972) under Part B of Medicare (covering physician, outpatient, and home health services) for the indigent aged as well as the sizable deductible and coinsurance liabilities under both Parts A (primarily hospitalization) and B, contributing over $325 million (1972) to the cost of hospital and ambulatory care for the aged. In addition, Medicaid made payments of $210 million (1972) for prescription drugs for the aged poor. Medicaid has financed a major expansion of nursing home care for the aged and chronically ill, with total payments to nursing homes of over $1.5 billion in 1972. In addition, the program has greatly increased the access of poor families as well as of blind and disabled persons to a wide variety of medical services. In many cases, medical services were previously financially inaccessible to such persons, or provided on a charity basis in often demeaning circumstances.

The distribution of Medicaid costs in 1970 by service and eligibility category can be seen in Table 2-1. The bulk of Medicaid funds support institutional services: 31.9 percent of Medicaid expenditures go for hospital inpatient care, while 28.3 percent is spent on nursing home care. Thirty-seven percent of Medicaid funds in 1970 were spent on behalf of the aged. This includes premiums, deductibles, and coinsurance for hospital inpatient and outpatient care and physician services under Medicare. The greatest portion of costs incurred by the aged goes to long-term care facilities: 58.7 percent of all Medicaid funds spent on the aged went to nursing homes. Next in importance for the aged was care in mental hospitals (13.5 percent) and prescriptions drugs (10.0 percent). The bulk of the remaining Medicaid funds was distributed among APTD (18.9 percent), AFDC-adults (18.6 percent), and AFDC-children (17.5 percent) recipients. The major service financed by Medicaid for these three groups was hospital inpatient care; hospital expenditures as a percentage of the total were 41.7 percent for the disabled, 40.8 percent for AFDC-children, and 51.7 percent for AFDC-adults. The second-ranking service for the disabled is nursing home care, which accounted for 24.9 percent of costs in 1970. Physician services followed inpatient care for AFDC adults and children, with 21.4 percent and 22.3 percent, respectively.

9

Table 2-1
Total Medicaid Expenditures by Type of Service and Eligibility Category, 1970 (in millions)

	Total	Aged	Blind	Disabled	AFDC Adults	AFDC Children	Other[3]
Total	$4,808.4	$1,783.7	$35.3	$994.5	$892.0	$841.7	$258.7
Hospital Inpatient	1,533.7 (31.9%)	129.8 (7.3%)	10.8 (31.0%)	414.7 (41.7%)	461.5 (51.7%)	343.0 (40.8%)	183.0 (70.7%)
Mental Hospital	308.2 (6.4%)	240.3 (13.5%)	0.6 (1.7%)	51.0 (5.1%)	0.7 (0.1%)	13.3 (1.6%)	2.3 (0.9%)
Nursing Home Services	1,362.1 (28.3%)	1,046.7 (58.7%)	9.5 (26.9%)	247.3 (24.9%)	6.0 (0.7%)	49.5 (5.9%)	3.1 (1.2%)
Physician Services[1]	616.6 (12.8%)	102.0 (5.7%)	5.3 (15.0%)	104.8 (10.5%)	191.3 (21.4%)	188.1 (22.3%)	25.1 (9.7%)
Dental Services	149.2 (3.1%)	18.2 (1.0%)	0.8 (2.3%)	16.1 (1.6%)	49.5 (5.5%)	57.5 (6.8%)	7.1 (2.7%)
Hospital Outpatient	221.5 (4.6%)	19.2 (1.1%)	1.3 (3.7%)	40.2 (4.0%)	60.4 (6.8%)	86.5 (10.3%)	14.0 (5.4%)
Prescribed Drugs	403.2 (8.4%)	179.0 (10.0%)	4.9 (13.9%)	80.5 (8.1%)	70.9 (7.9%)	52.3 (6.2%)	15.6 (6.0%)
Other[2]	122.2 (2.5%)	57.5 (3.2%)	2.1 (5.9%)	40.0 (4.0%)	51.8 (5.8%)	51.8 (6.1%)	8.4 (3.2%)

Source: U.S. Department of Health Education and Welfare, National Center for Social Statistics, *Numbers of Recipients and Amounts of Payments under Medicaid, 1970* (Washington, D.C. 1972).

[1] Physician Services include lab and X-ray totals.

[2] Other services include tuberculosis hospital care, other practitioners care, clinic services, home health services, and other care.

[3] Other eligibles include primarily general assistance cases, but may include some non-categorically related medically needy children.

While the contributions of Medicaid to the general health of the poor are undoubtedly many, there are several major problems with the program. The program can be criticized on both equity and efficiency grounds. Due to the nature of the program, with its federal-state sharing of costs, considerable inequities have developed. There are great differences among states in the percentage of the poor covered and in benefits provided. Some states will cover male-headed families; others will not. Some states will provide several optional benefits, such as prescription drugs and dental care; others will not. Some will cover the medically needy; others do not. The level of income families or individuals can have and remain eligible varies enormously among states. Schemes for reimbursing physicians—which affect their willingness to treat Medicaid eligibles—also vary considerably among states.

On efficiency grounds, the program can be criticized for lack of concern with creating incentives for both users and providers to use scarce resources rationally. As a result, Medicaid is vulnerable to arguments that it has contributed to medical care price inflation without adequately controlling the quality of care. Finally, it is often argued that the program contributes to the weakening of work incentives for the welfare population.

These equity and efficiency issues in Medicaid will be discussed in greater detail in the following pages. In addition an analysis of the growth in Medicaid costs over time will be presented. We attempt to show that, rather than being a program which is "out of control," Medicaid costs have largely risen because of increases in the number of public assistance recipients. Participation rates of eligibles have risen slightly, while use of services per eligible has largely been stable over time. Prices of services have risen over time, but Medicaid has probably been more a victim of this than a contributor.

Equity

Eligibility

All states which participate in Medicaid must cover those eligible for cash assistance programs (OAA, AB, APTD, AFDC). Eligibility for cash assistance is determined by a complex means test which differs by state. The primary determinant of eligibility is the standard of need calculated by each state based on its assessment of the requirements of a family of a given size with no other source of income. Cash assistance payments are made on the basis of some portion of the need standard determined for the recipient unit. Monthly payments depend on the family's non-assistance income less deductions. Some states use the full standard and pay the full budget deficit. Some, however, use a reduced standard and determine payments by comparing current resources to the reduced standard. Still others, using either the full or reduced standard, pay only a percentage of the budget deficit. In addition, some states place a maximum on the payment allowed.[a]

After disregarding a certain minimal level of income ($30 per month) and making an allowance for child care and other work-related expenses, a family's assistance payments are reduced by 67 cents for each dollar of earnings until payments equal zero at the "breakeven" point. The level of income a family can have and remain eligible for cash assistance and Medicaid will vary by state because the payment standard (the level of cash assistance payments if earned income is zero) and the amount of child care and work-related expenses permitted vary widely among states [49]. Cash assistance payments are deter-mined in general by the formula shown below [1, 7, 46]. In mathematical symbols, the welfare payment (P) may be defined as

$$P = r^d (S - Y^u - NEI) \tag{2.1}$$

where

P = payment

r^d = ratable reduction to the budget deficit, when applicable

S = effective standard (either the full or reduced standard)

NEI = non-exempt earned income

Y^u = unearned non-assistance income

Non-exempt earned income (NEI) is essentially gross earnings less the following deductions: one-third of gross earnings less $30 (monthly), and work-related and child care expenses.

$$NEI = .667 (Y^e - \$30) - WRE - CCE \tag{2.2}$$

---

[a]States which use the full standard and pay the full budget deficit are Connecticut, Colorado, Hawaii, Illinois, Massachusetts, Michigan, Minnesota, New Hampshire, New Jersey, North Dakota, South Dakota, Pennsylvania, Rhode Island, and Vermont.

States which use a reduced standard and pay the full deficit are the District of Columbia, Idaho, Iowa, Kansas, Louisiana, Maryland, Montana, New York, North Carolina, Ohio, Oklahoma, Oregon, Texas, Utah, West Virginia, and Wisconsin.

States which use the full standard but pay a percentage of the budget deficit are Arizona, Florida, and South Carolina.

The states of Alaska, California, Georgia, Indiana, Maine, Missouri, Nebraska, Tennessee, and Washington use a full standard and pay the full deficit, but limit payments to a maximum. Delaware, Kentucky, and Virginia pay a reduced standard and full deficit, and have a maximum payment. Alabama, Mississippi, New Mexico, and Wyoming pay a percentage of the budget deficit and limit payments to a maximum.

The payment method for Arkansas and Nevada were not specified in the source used here.

See U.S. Department of Health, Education and Welfare, Assistance Payments Administration, "Summary of Payment Methods," May 1971 (mimeographed).

where

.667 = marginal tax rate on earnings

Y^e = gross earnings

$30 = earnings disregard per month

WRE = work-related expenses

CCE = child care expenses

When the calculated NEI is less than zero, NEI is given a zero value in (2.1). In those states which specify a maximum payment, actual payments may not exceed that level. Families remain eligible for Medicaid as long as they remain eligible for cash assistance. The breakeven point (the level of earned income at which payments are reduced to zero) can be determined by setting $P = 0$ and solving for Y^e.

The variance in states' eligibility requirements for Medicaid coverage can best be illustrated by looking at state maximum payments. The maximum payments are made to those with no earned income, and cash assistance recipients tend to have little earned income rather than levels of income near the breakeven point [7]. Table 2-2 provides the maximum payment for each state. The payment level in the highest state, Connecticut, was more than five times that of the lowest, Mississippi. (By contrast, per capita income in Connecticut was less than twice that of Mississippi.)

In addition to those eligible because they are recipients of cash assistance, the following states also cover medically needy individuals not meeting cash assistance criteria: California, Connecticut, D.C., Hawaii, Illinois, Kansas, Kentucky, Maryland, Massachusetts, Michigan, Minnesota, Nebraska, New Hampshire, New York, North Carolina, North Dakota, Oklahoma, Pennsylvania, Rhode Island, Texas, Utah, Vermont, Virginia, Washington, and Wisconsin. As of 1967, the medically needy for all programs were limited to those whose income did not exceed 133-1/3 percent of the maximum payments for similar sized families under AFDC. This, of course, implies medical assistance for persons not eligible for cash assistance. At the same time, however, a family's total income under the cash assistance program can be greater than 133 percent of the maximum AFDC payment (see payments formula described above). Thus a family or individual eligible under the cash assistance program can have a higher total income than one eligible under the medically needy program and in many states may be eligible for more Medicaid-covered services.

Persons or families can also become eligible for medical assistance under the medically needy program if they have income above the 133-1/3 percent level but have high medical expenses which reduce income below the medically needy maximum. Through a provision known as the "spend-down," the program will pay all medical expenses which would reduce the after-tax income below the

Table 2-2
Maximum Annual Cash Assistance Payments for Four-Person Families, 1971, by State

Alabama	$ 972	Kentucky	$2,316	North Dakota	$3,600
Alaska	3,600	Lousiana	1,248	Ohio	2,400
Arizona	2,075	Maine	2,016	Oklahoma	2,268
Arkansas	1,212	Maryland	2,400	Oregon	2,688
California	3,360	Massachusetts	3,396	Pennsylvania	3,612
Colorado	2,820	Michigan	3,516	Rhode Island	3,060
Connecticut	4,020	Minnesota	3,708	South Carolina	1,236
Delaware	1,894	Mississippi	720	South Dakota	3,240
D.C.	2,934	Missouri	1,560	Tennessee	1,548
Florida	1,606	Montana	2,472	Texas	1,776
Georgia	1,788	Nebraska	2,712	Utah	2,688
Hawaii	3,216	Nevada	2,112	Vermont	3,828
Idaho	2,892	New Hampshire	3,768	Virginia	3,132
Illinois	3,276	New Jersey	3,888	Washington	3,240
Indiana	2,100	New Mexico	2,148	West Virginia	1,636
Iowa	2,916	New York	3,756	Wisconsin	2,604
Kansas	2,712	North Carolina	2,064	Wyoming	2,724

Source: U.S. Department of Health, Education and Welfare, Assistance Payments Administration, "Summary of Payment Methods," May 1971 (mimeographed).

medically needy maximum. For example, if a program has a medically needy maximum of $4,000, a family with income of $5,000 and medical expenses of $1,500 would have $500 paid by Medicaid. Clearly, families in states with medically needy programs could have quite large incomes and receive Medicaid payments under this catastrophic-protection provision.[b]

Prior to the passage of the 1972 Amendments to the Social Security Act, P.L. 92-603, the federal government would share administrative costs but not claims expenses for those who qualified for general assistance and those between twenty-one and sixty-five who were "medically needy" but did not fall into a categorically related definition. With the passage of the Social Security Amendments of 1972, the federal government will no longer contribute to the coverage of these groups. However, except for New York and Pennsylvania, few states

[b]There are two other categories of persons who may be included in the Medicaid program and for whom federal cost-sharing is available. The first category is called the categorically-related needy and includes those who could be covered by federal categorical programs if the state had adopted the broadest cash assistance programs permitted by the legislation and those who would be eligible for assistance if they were not in a medical institution. The second category is called the noncategorically-related medically needy and consists of those who were under twenty-one and medically "indigent" even if they were not eligible for another categorical program.

covered many persons not falling into the cash assistance or medically needy programs. The result is that single individuals and childless families are not covered, regardless of degree of indigency. (This is true, of course, only if such persons are not eligible for one of the adult aid programs.) Finally, in many states members of male-headed families are also not covered. In 1971, only twenty-five states made payments to families with unemployed fathers.

The net result of the wide variations in eligibility criteria is that the distribution of Medicaid expenditures among the poor is grossly uneven, as is readily discernible from Table 2-3. The Medicaid program covers most of the poor and many of the near poor in some states, while covering but a small percentage of the poor in others. The responsibility for this result lies principally with the initial design of the program, which tied it to the existing welfare system, rather than with the administration of the program at the federal or state level.

Table 2-3 provides an indication of the uneven coverage by Medicaid of the nation's poor. The table contains the numbers of users of services under Medicaid and the ratios of Medicaid recipients to persons under the poverty line and to persons under 125 percent of the poverty line. Ratios are provided for persons both under sixty-five and over sixty-five. The ratio of Medicaid recipients to all persons under sixty-five below the Census poverty line was .078 in Arkansas, .085 in Texas, .096 in Mississippi, and .103 in Alabama. On the other hand, the same ratio was 1.700 in New York, 1.500 in California, and 1.110 in Pennsylvania. With respect to persons over sixty-five, the ratio of users of services under Medicaid to persons under the poverty line varies from .187 in West Virginia and .192 in Arkansas to 3.170 in California, 1.340 in Colorado, and 1.300 in Rhode Island.

While Table 2-3 strongly suggests that inequities exist, some caution must be exercised in the interpretation. For example, a ratio equal to unity could mean that services are received by no one above the poverty line but by all of those below it, or that many above the line received services, but several persons below the line did not require services during the year. Likewise, ratios greater than unity reflect coverage of many persons above the poverty line as well as presumably a high proportion of those below. Where ratios are less than one, many persons who are recipients of services under Medicaid may be above the poverty line. Because of generous welfare standards or because of the method of calculating eligibility under the cash assistance programs, individuals with substantial earned income can be eligible for Medicaid. Because of participation by persons above the poverty line, these ratios may be biased upward as indicators of the success of the program in financing care for the poor. On the other hand, in any state there are an unknown number of persons who do not require health care services in a given year; that is, there is no a priori reason why, under say a generous national program with uniform eligibility criteria, 100 percent of persons under the poverty line would be users of services.

Table 2-3
Variations in Medicaid Coverage of the Poor, 1970

	Medicaid Users Under 65	Ratio of Medicaid Users to Persons Under 65 Below Pov. Level	Ratio of Medicaid Users to Persons Under 65 Below .125% Pov. Level	Medicaid Users Age 65+	Ratio of Medicaid Users to Persons 65+ Below Pov. Level	Ratio of Medicaid Users to Persons 65+ Below .125% Poverty Level
Alabama	74,054	.103	.080	69,907	.494	.404
Arkansas	32,417	.078	.059	20,631	.192	.156
California	2,767,000	1.500	1.090	982,800	3.170	2.070
Colorado	100,060	.457	.327	59,628	1.340	1.020
Connecticut	134,579	.810	.586	23,441	.509	.373
Delaware	32,830	.680	.485	2,755	.279	.212
D.C.	102,805	.943	.707	9,470	.675	.544
Florida	188,631	.221	.161	100,304	.427	.319
Georgia	218,379	.280	.211	103,415	.713	.589
Hawaii	57,574	.958	.637	8,120	.963	.727
Idaho	19,518	.270	.179	5,058	.262	.194
Indiana	530,357	.615	.451	84,365	.339	.257
Iowa	85,696	.379	.258	29,665	.321	.237
Kansas	99,282	.487	.331	25,476	.356	.266
Kentucky	218,752	.372	.286	89,033	.685	.552
Louisiana	97,804	.122	.096	120,125	.940	.766
Maine	47,775	.471	.305	9,573	.321	.235
Maryland	249,713	.771	.549	42,634	.681	.519
Michigan	359,700	.554	.405	80,960	.470	.349
Minnesota	172,385	.581	.404	55,342	.548	.404
Mississippi	62,485	.096	.079	58,247	.493	.425
Missouri	166,082	.329	.237	91,619	.545	.407
Montana	20,062	.272	.184	5,527	.309	.230
Nebraska	43,767	.313	.214	18,974	.392	.296
Nevada	15,081	.408	.280	3,617	.555	.381
New Hampshire	19,425	.422	.268	9,737	.520	.386
New Jersey	299,860	.669	.471	28,031	.223	.164
New Mexico	55,260	.273	.205	9,153	.370	.299
New York	2,684,400	1.700	1.220	415,200	1.020	.755
North Dakota	15,910	.209	.144	6,665	.396	.298
Ohio	305,990	.383	.274	71,450	.294	.222
Oklahoma	142,750	.400	.226	68,982	.637	.491
Oregon	73,661	.403	.291	16,038	.308	.224

Table 2-3 (cont.)

	Medicaid Users Under 65	Ratio of Medicaid Users to Persons Under 65 Below Pov. Level	Ratio of Medicaid Users to Persons Under 65 Below .125% Pov. Level	Medicaid Users Age 65+	Ratio of Medicaid Users to Persons 65+ Below Pov. Level	Ratio of Medicaid Users to Persons 65+ Below .125% Poverty Level
Pennsylvania	1,032,092	1.110	.767	113,282	.382	.287
Rhode Island	64,110	.849	.615	31,926	1.300	1.000
South Carolina	65,800	.128	.097	29,974	.379	.317
South Dakota	13,696	.143	.101	6,717	.284	.216
Tennessee	110,730	.163	.121	50,525	.321	.266
Texas	145,901	.085	.062	214,608	.655	.511
Utah	44,151	.447	.309	9,677	.496	.372
Vermont	28,362	.707	.475	8,329	.724	.522
Virginia	111,717	.192	.139	30,355	.276	.222
Washington	232,420	.888	.642	49,100	.665	.478
West Virginia	117,921	.385	.289	13,890	.187	.149
Wisconsin	180,707	.576	.402	66,564	.623	.452
Wyoming	5,466	.178	.122	1,770	.245	.720

Source: Users –U.S. Department of Health, Education and Welfare, National Center for Social Statistics, *Numbers of Recipients and Amounts of Payments under Medicaid and Other Medical Programs Financed From Public Assistance Funds, 1970* (Washington, D.C.).

Poverty Data –U.S. Bureau of Census, Census of Population 1970, *General Social and Economic Characteristics*, Final Report (PC(1) - C1 United States Summary (Washington, D.C.: U.S. Government Printing Office, 1972.

High coverage ratios are generally due to coverage of persons with higher incomes (relative to states with low coverage ratios), coverage of the medically needy, coverage of male-headed families, provision of information about the program, and the greater availability of health care providers. High ratios in New York and Pennsylvania are in part due to coverage of persons receiving general assistance. It should be noted that because poverty lines vary only by family size, sex of family head, and farm or non-farm residence, and do not reflect cost-of-living differences among states or regions, relatively wealthy states can be providing coverage for fewer persons in need than a poor state with a lower coverage ratio.

Despite these considerations, the coverage of the poor under Medicaid appears to be more unequal than should be tolerated under a program which is more than 55 percent federally funded. A redistribution of expenditures from states which provide coverage for many individuals who are not poor under the Census definition towards the many individuals in other states who are would seem to be consistent with almost any notion of equity. In addition, such redistributions are very likely to increase the benefits (in terms of improved health of the poor) from federal expenditures. Universal coverage under a federal program, as is now suggested in several national health insurance plans before Congress, should succeed in bringing about a more equitable distribution of federal funds.

Benefits

The inequities described above are compounded when one looks at the medical services covered under Medicaid in different states. As of 1970, all states must provide inpatient and outpatient hospital services, physician services, laboratory and X-ray diagnostic services, skilled nursing home care, and home health services to the categorically needy as well as early and periodic screening, diagnosis, and treatment for categorically needy children under twenty-one. For the medically needy, states may provide the first six or any seven from among those listed above and private duty nursing services; clinic services; dental services; physical therapy and related services; prescribed drugs; dentures and prosthetic devices; inpatient hospital services and skilled nursing home services for individuals aged sixty-five and over in an institution for tuberculosis or mental diseases.

The variance in covered medical services benefits for both categorically needy and medically needy as of March 1971 is shown in Table 2-4. The first column (FMAP) gives the percentage of a state's medical vendor payment expenditures paid by the federal government. The second column indicates whether required services are provided for just cash assistance recipients (C) or for both cash assistance recipients and the medically needy (M). The remaining columns indicate which optional services are covered and for which groups. As shown in Table 2-4, several states provide most optional services for both cash assistance and medically needy recipients.[c] Many others cover most additional services for the cash assistance program only.[d] On the other hand, several others offer relatively few additional services to the cash assistance population.[e]

An estimate of the value of the Medicaid package to three categories of eligibles in the five highest and five lowest expenditure per capita states is shown in Table 2-5. These estimates, which were made for the non-institutionalized cash assistance population only, should not be interpreted strictly as actuarial values, but merely as indicators of the variance in outlays per eligible person

---

[c]California, Connecticut, Illinois, Kansas, Maryland, Massachusetts, Minnesota, Nebraska, New York, North Dakota, Utah, and Washington.

[d]Indiana, Maine, Nevada, New Jersey, Oregon, and West Virginia.

[e]Alabama, Arkansas, Florida, Georgia, Mississippi, Missouri, South Carolina, Wyoming, and Tennessee.

Table 2-4
Provisions of Optional Services Under Medicaid, 1972

	FMAP[1]	Required Services[2,3]	Optional Services[4]																	
			1	2	3	4	5	6	7	8	9	10	11	12	13	14	15	16	17
Alabama	78	C		C			C				C			C					C	C[5]
Arkansas	79	C		C	C						C							C	C	C
California	50	M	M	M	M	M	M	M	M		M	M	M	M	M	C	M	M	M
Colorado	58	C		C	M	C						C	C	M	C	M	C		C
Connecticut	50	M	M	M	M	M	M	M	M	M	C	M	M	M	M		M		
Delaware	50	C	C	C		C			C	C		C	C		C	M	C	C	
D.C.	50	M	M	M	M	M	M		M		M	M	M	M	M		M	M	M
Florida	61	C		C							C	C	C				C	C	C
Georgia	70	C		C								C	C		C				
Hawaii	51	M	M	M	M	M	M	M	M	M	M	M	M	M			M	M[5]
Idaho	72	C		C								C	C	C	C	C	C	C
Illinois	50	M	M	M	M	M	M	M	M	M	M	M	M	M	C	M		M
Indiana	55	C	C	C	C	C	C	C	C	C	C	C	C	C			M	C[5]
Iowa	58	C	C	C	C	C	C	C	C	C	C	C	C	C	C			
Kansas	59	M	M	M	M	M	M	M	M	M	M	M	M	M	C	M	M	M
Kentucky	73	M	M	M	M				M	M		M	M				M	M	C[5]
Louisiana	73	C	C	C		C	C	C	C	C	C	C		C		C	C	C[5]
Maine	69	C	C	C		C	C	M	M	C	C	C	C	C	C	C		C[5]
Maryland	50	M	M	M	M	M	M	M	M	M	M	M	M	M		M	M	M[5]
Massachusetts	50	M	M	M	M	M	M	M	M		M	M	M	M	M	M	M	M[5]
Michigan	50	M	M	M	M		M	M	M	M	M	M	M		M	M	M	M
Minnesota	57	M	M	M	M	M	M	M	M	M	M	M	M	M	M	M	M	M

Table 2-4 (cont.)

	FMAP[1]	Required Services[2],[3]	Optional Services[4]																
			1	2	3	4	5	6	7	8	9	10	11	12	13	14	15	16	17
Mississippi	83	C		C	C	C	C				C		C	C				C	C
Missouri	60	C	C	C	C							C	C				C	C	C
Montana	67	C	C	C	C	C	C	C	C		C	C	C	C	M	M	C	C	C
Nebraska	58	M	M	M	M	M	M	M	M	M	M	M	M	M	M	M	M	M	M
Nevada	50	C	C	C	C	C	C	C	C	C	C	C	C	C	C		C	C	C[5]
New Hampshire	59	M	M	M	M	C	M	C	C	C	M	M	M	M	C	M	C		
New Jersey	50	C	C	C	C	C	C		C	C	C	C	C	C	C		C	C	C
New Mexico	73	C	C	C	C	C	C		C	C	C	C	C	C	C				C
New York	50	M	M	M	M	M	M	M	M	M	M	M	M	M	M	M	M	M	M
North Carolina	73	M		M	M	M	M	M	M	M	M	M	M		M	M	C		M	
North Dakota	71	M	M	M	M	M	M	M	C		M	M	M	M	M	M	M	M	
Ohio	54	C	C	C		C	C	C	C	C	C	C	C	C	C	C	C		C
Oklahoma	69	M			M									M				M	M
Oregon	57	C	C	C	C	C	C	C	C	C	C	C	C	C	C		M	C	C	C
Pennsylvania	55	M	M	C	C	C	M						C	M	M	C	M	M		C
Rhode Island	50	M		M	M	M	M						M		M	M		M		C
South Carolina	78	C	C	C							C		C	C	C		C	C	C
South Dakota	70	C	C			C	C		C		C	C	C		C	C			C[5]
Tennessee	74	C		C		C				C		C		C	C	C	C		C
Texas	65	C		C										C	C	C	C	C	C
Utah	70	M	M	M	M	M	M	M	M	M	M	M	M	M	M	M	M	M	M
Vermont	65	M	M	M	M	M	M	M	M	M	M	M	M		M		M	M	M[5]

Virginia	64	M	M	M		M	M		M		M	M	M	M	M		M	M	M
Washington	50	M	M	M	M	M	M	M	M	M	M	M	M	M	M	M	M	M	M
West Virginia	77	C	C	C	C	C	C	C	C	C		C	C	C	C	C	C	C	
Wisconsin	58	M	M	M	M	C	C	C	M	C	M		C	C	M		M		M
Wyoming	63	C																	C[5]

Source: U.S. Department of Health, Education and Welfare, National Center for Social Statistics, mimeograph.

1. FMAP–Federal Medical Assistance Percentage: rate of federal financial participation in a state's medical vendor payment expenditures on behalf of individuals and families eligible under Title XIX of Social Security Act. Percentages effective from July 1, 1971, through June 30, 1973 are rounded.

2. Required Services: (1) inpatient hospital services; (2) outpatient hospital services; (3) other laboratory and X-ray services; (4) skilled nursing home services for individuals aged 21 or older; (5) physician services; (6) early and periodic screening, diagnosis and treatment of individuals under the age of 21; and (7) home health care services for any individual entitled to skilled nursing home services.

3. C–offered for persons receiving federally supported financial assistance; M–offered also for persons in public assistance categories who are financially eligible for medical but not financial assistance.

4. Optional Services for which federal financial participation is available.

5. Does not include ICF services in institutions for the mentally retarded.

1. Clinic services
2. Prescribed Drugs
3. Dental services
4. Prosthetic devices
5. Eyeglasses
6. Private duty nursing
7. Physical therapy and related services
8. Other diagnostic, screening, preventive, and rehabilitative services
9. Emergency hospital services
10. Family planning services
11. Skilled nursing home services
12. Optometrists' services
13. Podiatrists' services
14. Chiropractors' services
15. Care of patients 65 and over in institutions for mental diseases
16. Care of patients 65 or older in institutions for tuberculosis
17. Institutional services in intermediate care facilities

Table 2-5
Variations in Medicaid Expenditures Per Eligible, 1970 Cash Assistance Recipients

	Required Services		Optional Services		Total Services	
	Highest	Lowest	Highest	Lowest	Highest	Lowest
Disabled						
	New York $932.91	Arkansas $105.31	California $294.80	Idaho $ 3.07	California $1116.34	Arkansas $109.77
	Wisconsin 920.59	Mississippi 120.53	Minnesota 201.72	Arkansas 4.46	Wisconsin 1114.82	Mississippi 146.06
	Minnesota 850.88	Tennessee 143.40	Wisconsin 194.23	S. Dakota 13.04	Minnesota 1052.60	Tennessee 201.43
	California 821.54	West Virginia 187.94	Kansas 192.48	Oklahoma 13.84	New York 999.78	Louisiana 244.85
	Michigan 674.44	Louisiana 199.22	N. Hampshire 187.57	Mississippi 25.53	Connecticut 781.58	W. Virginia 246.21
AFDC–Children						
	Vermont $119.64	Mississippi $10.15	New York $43.30	Louisiana $ .44	Vermont $141.76	Mississippi $12.15
	Illinois 89.30	Arkansas 15.45	Minnesota 33.25	Idaho .67	Minnesota 111.13	Arkansas 17.16
	Connecticut 78.48	Louisiana 17.57	N. Hampshire 31.48	Arkansas 1.71	Illinois 110.46	Oregon 21.84
	Minnesota 77.88	Oregon 17.89	Connecticut 22.14	Mississippi 2.00	Connecticut 100.62	Florida 23.67
	Rhode Island 76.15	Tennessee 21.21	Vermont 22.12	Florida 2.09	New York 96.86	Tennessee 24.58
AFDC–Adult						
	New York $298.07	Arkansas $49.54	Minnesota $88.28	Idaho $ 1.74	Wisconsin $366.96	Arkansas $ 53.56
	Wisconsin 293.54	Tennessee 70.05	Iowa 78.78	Oklahoma 1.87	New York 352.90	Louisiana 82.10
	Nevada 269.94	Louisiana 74.17	Kansas 78.64	Arkansas 4.03	Minnesota 336.72	Tennessee 90.39
	D.C. 252.16	New Jersey 77.71	Wisconsin 73.42	Louisiana 7.93	Kansas 326.66	Oregon 95.90
	Minnesota 248.44	Oregon 85.70	N. Hampshire 71.50	S. Dakota 9.44	Illinois 308.96	New Jersey 104.85

Source: Expenditures data is reported annually by the states to the National Center for Social Statistics. Summary statistics are published in *Numbers of Recipients and Amounts of Payments under Medicaid and Other Medical Programs Financed from Public Assistance Funds,* 1969. Estimates of eligibles were developed from various public assistance publications. The method of estimating eligibles is described in Appendix A.

across states. Expenditure data for each service is reported annually by each state to the National Center for Social Statistics. Estimates of eligibles were made from data on public assistance caseloads and case openings and closings (see Appendix A). Unfortunately, the expenditure data include expenditures made on behalf of both full- and part-year eligibles. The estimates of eligibles correspond to this by including any person who was eligible at any time during the year.[f]

The variance in program benefits across states in all aid categories is quite large. Some of the variance can be explained by differences in optional services covered. While the variance in optional services is quite large, outlays on optional services is low even in high expenditure states. Thus, it is clear that most of the variance in total expenditures per eligible person is explained by differences in per capita outlays on required services. Further examination of the data (see Appendix B) on specific services indicates that there is great variance both in the percentage of eligibles who use particular services and in expenditures per user of the service. Expenditures per user will, of course, reflect the prices and quality as well as the number of services.

It is not surprising that the wealthy states have high expenditures per eligible or that the relatively poor states have low expenditures. It is surprising that the variations are so large. It appears that the lowest federal matching rate (50 percent) in wealthy states is sufficient incentive to ensure a generous program, while relatively high federal matching in poor states—the maximum is 83 percent—is not sufficient to induce those states to provide more than a basic minimum level of services. In Chapters 3 and 4, an effort is made to explain the causes of variation in state expenditures. We examine the influence of reimbursement arrangements, the geographic distribution of health service providers, income, education, race, and other factors on service utilization.

Efficiency

Price Inflation

Under the structure of the Medicaid program there is a virtual absence of incentives for either consumers or providers to use scarce resources efficiently. Unlike Medicare, all services under Medicaid are provided free of charge to the user.[g] Because of the poverty status of the eligible population it was deemed

---

[f]Expenditures per eligible will, therefore, be influenced by caseload turnover. In Chapter 4 we provide evidence that the turnover rate is inversely related to service utilization; however, this relationship is often not statistically significant. Thus, variance in turnover rates among states will not greatly affect the expenditure per eligible estimates.

[g]Beginning January 1, 1973 states were permitted to employ nominal charges on all services for the medically needy and on optional services for cash assistance recipients.

unjust or unfair to impose any system of cost sharing. It is also argued that a system of deductibles and coinsurance payments which discourage unnecessary utilization but did not discourage valuable services would also be difficult to administer and a burden to providers. As a result, there is no incentive for the eligible person to avoid using services of little medical value. There is also no incentive for consumers to make choices among alternative providers on the basis of price and thus little incentive for providers to compete in the delivery of care. However, with few exceptions, no alternative mechanism for monitoring consumer demand has been substituted and, at the same time, there have been few controls on provider behavior.

Medicaid is a public program which operates by purchasing services from the private sector. The objective in this situation is to purchase necessary services at satisfactory quality levels at reasonable prices. Defining necessary services, satisfactory quality levels and reasonable prices for subsidized services is, of course, extremely difficult. However, there is reason to believe that under Medicaid the quantity and quality of services have often been excessive and that the program has contributed to medical care price increases. Part of the problem of analyzing subsidized services is that there are equally numerous cases of provision of insufficient services and examples of care of mediocre quality. This can occur either because Medicaid authorities in the various states are unwilling to pay the requisite price for services at satisfactory quality levels or because consumers are unable to make accurate judgements about the quality of available providers due to a lack of reliable information.

The mechanism through which Medicaid purchases services from two types of providers is worthy of discussion, with emphasis on the way the purchase of services contributes to price increases.

Hospitals. The mechanism through which increased demand has been translated into higher hospital prices has been described by several authors. M. Feldstein has argued that hospitals react to increased demand by raising prices because of internal pressures for quality enhancement rather than to increase profits. [16]. The medical and professional staff press for advanced facilities and equipment and sophisticated ancillary services. Administrators are concerned with increasing the quality of patient care through improving the level of patient amenities. Finally, the hospital is faced with a demand for higher wages and salaries by both professional and non-professional staff. Pressures for higher costs per patient day are constrained only by the need to cover costs with revenues (including philanthropic support). However, the increase in demand permits hospitals to yield to internal pressure.

It is not merely demand but the reimbursement mechanism as well which has caused rising hospital prices. Most hospitals are paid for services on a full cost reimbursement basis. Reasonable costs usually include labor, materials, bad debts, depreciation, and interest. By covering all costs, there is little incentive for a hospital to choose the socially optimal scale of operation or socially optimal input combinations. Full cost reimbursement permits the provision of additional services, the purchase of new equipment and hiring of additional personnel as long as a general increase in hospital rates will cover the additional expenditure. There is no necessity for the costs of new inputs to be matched by increases in revenue generated by the services produced by the new inputs. That is, new inputs do not have to be justified on the basis of demand for the services sufficient to pay for them. New equipment and personnel can be acquired and new services provided so long as their costs can be spread over hospital prices in general. The result is an over-allocation of resources to the hospital sector and excessive prices for routine services [28].

The normal market reaction to higher prices (increase in supply and decline in demand) is constrained by the non-profit status of most hospitals and by consumer indifference [32]. Because the industry is dominated by non-profit hospitals, higher prices do not attract new, more efficient producers or induce cost-reducing innovations in existing facilities. Because of the need to maintain status or prestige in the medical community in order to attract physicians and patients, it is difficult for a hospital to attempt to compete for patients by providing a lower quality, lower priced service. Finally, with third party coverage of all or most of the hospital charges, and the physician largely in control of the admission, discharge, and choice of facility decisions, consumers have little incentive or ability to restrain price increases.

Physicians. Reimbursement of physicians operates in a manner somewhat similar to that for hospitals. In most states reimbursements are on the basis of "reasonable" or "customary and usual" charges with limits set at specified levels. This method of reimbursement also generates strong pressure toward price inflation. Not all states, of course, have generous reimbursement schemes. Restrictive fee schedules do, in fact, control prices in several states. Clearly, at some level, controls can produce adverse effects on the quantity and quality of services provided Medicaid clients.

The first difficulty with "usual and customary fees" is that once the maximum fee level is set and becomes widely known, there is no reason for physicians to charge covered patients below that level. It tends soon to become the minimum fee. Further increases in charges over time to covered and uncovered patients lead to reestablishment of usual and customary fees at higher levels. Because services are free to Medicaid patients, they have no incentive to make choices among alternative physicians on the basis of price. While competition for uncovered patients would seem to restrain the pressure on prices, this effect probably does not operate too powerfully. Since the elasticity of demand for physician services seems to be less than unity [18, 21], increases in price have little effect on quantity demanded and result primarily in increases in physician incomes. The private market also becomes less important as insurance coverage of medical services increases. Consumers also have great difficulty determining the quality of services of physicians; thus price differentials may often be interpreted as quality differentials.

As long as prices paid under Medicaid are above the cost of service delivery, services desired by Medicaid eligibles should be provided. Physicians may respond to the prices paid by Medicaid by recommending additional diagnostic work and follow-up visits and increasing output through working longer hours, employing paramedical aides, etc. Expansion of services is not the only result one might expect, however. Due to the barriers to entry in medical practice, high fees may increase physician incomes but have little effect on output. Physicians may also respond to fees above their input costs by expanding the quality of their practice, which in turn increases the average cost of a given quantity of service [18, 23]. Finally, fees above input costs may also lead to inefficient use of inputs without affecting quality. That is, third party coverage can also permit duplication of facilities, excess manpower and excessive wage and salary increases in physician practices.

Quality of Care

Criticism of Medicaid has been by no means limited to excessive utilization and quality. One of the problems in setting public prices for private services is that such prices can be set too low. In fact, the Medicaid program has been frequently criticized for fostering and maintaining a dual system of medical care in which the program eligibles receive inferior treatment. Critics cite long waiting lines, unavailability of appointments, provider indifference, lack of comprehensiveness and continuity of care, unsanitary conditions, and insufficient numbers of skilled personnel in nursing homes and municipal hospitals. Some of these problems are not directly the fault of Medicaid. Medicaid eligibles, like the rest of the population, are affected by inefficiencies in the delivery system and by the maldistribution of health care resources. On the other hand, low reimbursement rates coupled with delays in payment and high claims-processing costs will affect the quality of care in some areas by reducing provider participation and decreasing the time spent per patient. It is also likely that, as a result of restrictive reimbursement arrangements, it may not be economically worthwhile for highly skilled practitioners to participate in the program, leaving the market to relatively low skilled providers.

Work Incentives

The welfare system has long been criticized for constructing significant barriers to work effort by maintaining high marginal tax rates. As mentioned earlier, welfare recipients lose 67 cents of public assistance payments for each dollar of earnings. At some point as earnings increased, public assistance payments are reduced to zero. At this "breakeven point" families or individuals also face the loss of several hundred dollars of medical benefits. This provision results in obvious disincentives to working one's way off the public assistance rolls. It also provides strong incentives to families facing high future medical expenses to cease working and apply for public assistance.

The Growth in the Cost of Medicaid

A major concern with the Medicaid program has been high and rapidly rising budget costs. The annual cost of the program has risen from less than $2.0 billion in 1966 to $8.0 billion in 1972. Expenditures have risen at annual rates of over 24 percent for the aged, 34 percent for the disabled, and 36 percent for families with dependent children, between 1967 and 1972. The rapid growth in Medicaid costs has placed severe pressures on budgets at both the federal and state levels. Rising public assistance and Medicaid expenditures have been partially responsible for eliminating the expected federal budget surplus and for tax increases in several states.

It is often alleged that the growth in Medicaid outlays is due to increased medical care prices which are the predictable outcome of a governmentally induced shift in demand in the face of an inelastic supply. However, while prices have risen during this period, they have not been the major cause of the growth in Medicaid. Rather, the number of persons eligible for the program has grown at a much faster rate than prices or any other factor.

To analyze the growth of Medicaid costs, we examined three mutually exclusive components of that growth: the number of eligibles, the participation rate of eligibles, and expenditures per user of services. Expenditures (X) is equal to the product of eligibles (E), the participation rate of eligibles (R/E), and expenditures per recipient (X/R).

The arithmetic expression for expenditures, then, is as follows:

$$X = E \cdot \frac{R}{E} \cdot \frac{X}{R} \tag{2.3}$$

The growth rate of expenditures is equal to the product of the growth rates of eligibles, the participation rate of eligibles and expenditures per recipient. The growth rate for each term in Equation (2.3) can be estimated with simple least squares regressions,[h] thereby determining the growth rate for each.

Calculations were made for the aged (OAA), disabled (APTD), and families

---

[h]For example, the regression equation used to obtain the growth rate of eligibles would be of the form: $\log E = a + bT$.

with dependent children (AFDC) groups. Each group is composed of those for whom money payments were authorized and for whom money payments were not authorized. The first category consists of those who were receiving cash assistance. The second category includes the medically needy as well as those who are eligible for cash assistance but refuse it and those who are in institutions, such as homes for the disabled and aged. For the cash assistance groups (for whom money payments were authorized), data were available on expenditures and recipients of Medicaid services for the middle month of each quarter as well as on eligibles by month. For our purposes, eligibles for Medicaid services under the cash assistance category include all persons receiving public assistance; "eligibles" excludes persons not receiving public assistance but who nonetheless could be because of income, family status, etc. Because of the spend-down feature of the medically needy category, it was impossible to determine eligibles for the group for whom money payments were not authorized. Thus recipients were used in place of eligibles. In the cash assistance categories, participation rates were formed by the simple division of recipients by eligibles (R/E).

The results are presented in Table 2-6. Each term indicates the estimated long-run average quarterly growth rate for the relevant component. An asterisk indicates the growth rate was statistically significant at the 0.5 percent level. The numbers in parentheses are the average annual growth rates, while the percentages given in brackets give the contribution of each component to the growth in expenditures.

Eligibles

The dominant contributor to the growth of expenditures in most categories was the increase in the number of Medicaid eligibles. The number of eligibles grew at the rate of 5.5 percent per quarter for the AFDC cash assistance population, the largest category in the program. The increase in eligibles accounted for almost 70 percent of the increase in expenditures in that group. The increase in eligibles also accounted for well over 50 percent of the growth in expenditures in the disabled cash assistance group and in the aged and disabled "money payments not authorized" groups.

Several reasons can be cited for the growth in AFDC caseloads. First, most states significantly increased their standards of need during this period. Furthermore, work incentive features introduced in 1969, the income disregard and deductions for work-related expenses, served to increase the breakeven point, thereby increasing the number of eligibles. A second factor is the growth in population, particularly the growth in female-headed families. Third, other program regulations have been liberalized. These would include the requirement that individuals be residents of a state for one year to be eligible for assistance

Table 2-6
The Growth of Medicaid Costs, 1967-1972

| | Money Payments Authorized | | | |
	Expenditures	Eligibles	Participation	Expenditures Per User
OAA	5.7* (24.8)	1.8* (7.5) [31.5%]	2.3* (9.5) [42.1%]	1.5* (6.1) [26.4%]
APTD	7.7* (34.5)	4.5* (19.2) [61.0%]	1.3* (5.3) [16.9%]	1.7* (7.0) [22.1%]
AFDC	8.1* (36.6)	5.4* (23.4) [67.9%]	1.5* (6.1) [18.5%]	1.1* (4.5) [13.6%]

| | Money Payments Not Authorized | | |
	Expenditures	Recipients	Expenditures Per User
OAA	4.5* (19.2)	2.4* (10.0) [53.3%]	2.1* (8.7) [46.7%]
APTD	7.0* (31.1)	5.0* (21.5) [72.8%]	1.9* (7.8) [27.2%]
AFDC	2.9* (12.1)	0.9* (3.7) [31.0%]	2.0* (8.2) [69.0%]

Sources:

1. Medicaid Recipients and Payments—U.S. Department of Health, Education and Welfare, National Center for Social Statistics. *Medical Assistance Financed under Title XIX of the Social Security Act.* Report B-1. February 1967 through December 1972.

2. Eligibles—U.S. Department of Health, Education and Welfare. Social and Rehabilitation Services. *Public Assistance Statistics.* National Center for Social Statistics. February 1967 through December 1972.

3. CPI—U.S. Department of Labor. Bureau of Labor Statistics. *The Consumer Price Index.* Table I. February 1967 through December 1972.

Note: (a) the first term is the estimated average quarterly growth rate
(b) an asterisk indicates the estimated growth rate is statistically significant at the .05 level
(c) the term in parentheses is the estimate of the average annual growth rate
(d) the term in brackets is the percentage of growth in expenditures attributable to the relevant component.

and the elimination of the man-in-the-house rule. Fourth, there was an increase in information about rights to public assistance through various poverty programs, the Food Stamp program, and groups such as the National Welfare Rights Organization. A final source of growth in Medicaid AFDC eligibles during this period has been the entrance of new states into the program.

The APTD (disabled) caseloads increased at a rapid rate as well. The increase in Medicaid eligibles averaged 4.7 percent per quarter which contributed to over 60 percent of the growth in expenditures. The increase in the need standard for the APTD program and the liberalization of the definition of disability both contributed to this growth. Another factor was the growth in importance of the

Disability Trust Fund. As the number of individuals receiving disability benefits from Social Security increased, information about the availability of health benefits under Medicaid spread.

The growth in eligibles was not as important for the aged on public assistance. The primary reason for growth in OAA eligibles for Medicaid was the entrance of new states into the program. There was also an increase in eligibles from the natural growth in population and the increase in public assistance benefit levels. But this was dampened considerably by the increase in minimum Social Security benefits which raised incomes in many states beyond public assistance need standards, thereby leaving such individuals ineligible for Medicaid.

It is more difficult to suggest reasons for the growth in recipients of services for the medically needy and others not authorized for cash assistance. One reason may be the growth in nursing homes and intermediate care facilities during this period [2]. Utilization of long-term care has grown along with the increase in these facilities [57]. The number of persons becoming eligible through the spend-down provision may have increased with the growth in available facilities. Persons not receiving cash assistance because they are in institutions may have increased for the same reason. Other factors include information spreading through the Food Stamp program and through medical care providers. Finally, medically needy recipients have also increased as states have entered the program throughout the period.

Participation

The participation rate of eligibles in the cash assistance categories increased at rates which averaged 1.3 percent per quarter for the disabled, 1.5 percent per quarter for AFDC, and 2.4 percent per quarter for the aged. The participation rate is defined as the percentage of eligibles using services each quarter. The growth in the participation rate may reflect a "learning" process. As people become aware of the availability and value of various services, the propensity to use increases. Under this hypothesis, the rate of increase would peak and then decline as "learning" loses importance. This view is supported by the observed decline in the rate of growth. A less benign interpretation would be that the increase in the percentage of eligibles using services each quarter reflects overutilization, a result of the lack of incentives to use services appropriately.

Expenditures Per Recipient

Expenditures per recipient of services grew at rates of 1.1 to 1.7 percent per quarter for public assistance recipients and at approximately 2.0 percent per quarter for those not authorized for public assistance. Some of this increase is due to rising prices and the remainder to changes in service utilization.

Prices. The medical care component of the Consumer Price Index grew at the rate of 6.4 percent per year during the period examined. The medical care price index may not be the appropriate deflator for Medicaid expenditures, however. It may understate the rise in prices paid by Medicaid in various states because physicians changed from sliding fee scales to higher levels of reimbursement. Whether the adjustment in pricing was immediate or if a significant amount of time elapsed before fees reached Medicaid permitted levels is unknown. On the other hand, the increase in prices may be overstated by the medical care price index if Medicaid, through fee schedules and other cost control measures, limited the rate of increase in its prices below that experienced nationally during the period. The estimate of the increase in prices will also be biased if the composition of services used by Medicaid eligibles differs from that used by the rest of the population.

The introduction and growth of Medicaid coverage has undoubtedly contributed to the severe inflationary pressures in the health care sector, both because of the increase in the number of individuals with complete insurance coverage and because of the lack of efficiency-generating incentives discussed in the previous section. However, it seems likely that Medicaid has been as much a victim of rising prices as a contributor, and perhaps more so. While efficiency-generating incentives have generally been lacking in the Medicaid program, they are also absent from the third party coverage of the rest of the nation. Because Medicaid finances care for less than 10 percent of the population it seems reasonable to assume that the principal impetus for the continued growth in prices comes from forces in the market.

Services. If the medical care price deflator reflects the rate of price inflation experienced by Medicaid, services per recipient were roughly constant for all groups. If the price deflator overstates the rate of increase in prices, then the growth in services is underestimated, and vice versa. Furthermore, if the composition of services used by Medicaid eligibles is more heavily weighted (than the rest of the population) with services whose prices increased faster than the medical care price index, the growth rate estimates for services will be even more overstated, and vice versa.

Constant or slightly declining use of services suggests that assertions of an uncontrollable program are misleading. One might speculate that in the beginning stages of the program, eligibles receive care for previously undiagnosed or untreated ailments. Following high use in initial periods, service needs decline. It is also likely that as participation rates increase, service needs, on average, are less frequent and less expensive. Thus, services per user would decline over time. Such declines are perhaps counterbalanced by increased use in particular services, primarily nursing home care.

Conclusion

From the evidence provided above, it appears that it is not at all inevitable that costs of a program of subsidized care for the poor escalate at rates approaching those under the current Medicaid program. The Medicaid experience has largely been the result of the initial design of the program which tied it to the growth of public assistance, and not merely the predictable outcome of subsidization. The most important factor in the rise of costs of Medicaid has been the increase in persons eligible. Under a continuation of the present Medicaid program, increases in the number of eligibles would be a much less important factor because public assistance caseloads are stabilizing [7] and all but one state is currently participating in Medicaid. A program with broad population coverage would avoid the problem of continually rising costs because, while large increases in eligibility and utilization would occur following the initial expansion of coverage, they would not continue over time. On the other hand, one would expect participation rates to increase just as in the Medicaid experience. Broadened coverage would also increase inflationary pressure, but alternative methods of reimbursing providers and alternative approaches to the financing and delivery of care could do much to mitigate such price effects (see Chapter 6).

3

Hospital Inpatient Care

Introduction

In this chapter we explore the causes of variations among states in expenditures per eligible person on hospital inpatient care. In the process we attempt to determine the influence on hospital utilization of certain variables which can, at least in theory, be manipulated by public policy. These include reimbursement arrangements, bed and physician availability, and incomes. It can be seen from Table 3-1 that hospital expenditures per eligible person vary widely by state. For the disabled, expenditures per eligible vary from over $400 in California and Rhode Island to under $100 in Mississippi and Arkansas. For AFDC children, expenditures per eligible ranged from over $50 in Illinois and the District of Columbia to under $10 in Arkansas and Mississippi. Finally, expenditures per eligible varied from over $200 in New York to under $50 in Tennessee and Arkansas for AFDC adults.[a]

The possible reasons for these widely differing outlays are many. Prices of hospital bed days vary widely across states, ranging from $52 in Wyoming to $101 in Connecticut. Hospital beds per capita range from 22.5 per 10,000 persons in Rhode Island to 72.0 per 10,000 persons in the District of Columbia. The number of active practicing physicians per 10,000 persons varies from 30.8 in the District of Columbia and 19.7 in New York to 7.3 in South Dakota and 7.4 in Mississippi. The availability of specialists who are more prone to provide care in hospital settings also varies widely by state. The manner in which physicians are reimbursed for services differs by state, varying from rather generous usual and customary fees to much more restrictive fee schedules. The needs of the eligible population, such as reflected in degree of disability, women in childbearing years, etc., will also vary. Finally, access to ambulatory care varies widely, and lack of access to ambulatory services may ultimately be reflected in hospital utilization rates. The racial and urban-rural composition as well as incomes of Medicaid eligible populations vary greatly across states. Non-whites, residents of rural areas, and those with low incomes are all alleged to very often find ambulatory care inaccessible in practice.

---

[a]As in Chapter 2, these estimates are not actuarial values of hospital benefits but rather indicators of the variance across states. Eligibles are defined to include all who are eligible at any time during the year and thus expenditures per eligible can vary with caseload turnover. However, the regression results described below indicate that turnover is not unimportant in explaining variance in expenditures per eligible.

Table 3-1
Hospital Inpatient Care, Expenditures Per Eligible, By State, 1970

	Disabled	AFDC Children	AFDC Adults
New England			
Maine	372.85	32.21	109.96
New Hampshire	402.26	22.18	117.53
Vermont	222.49	76.22	1. 106.74
Massachusetts	N/A	N/A	N/A
Rhode Island	432.64	45.27	137.79
Connecticut	415.48	48.34	140.29
Middle Atlantic			
New York	327.05	12.41	206.52
New Jersey	205.62	25.74	40.06
Pennsylvania	293.82	44.04	150.32
East North Central			
Ohio	375.80	32.02	131.01
Indiana	247.24	15.54	80.79
Illinois	371.01	57.95	157.75
Michigan	376.30	28.11	133.43
Wisconsin	321.48	32.45	165.29
West North Central			
Minnesota	388.19	40.93	153.22
Iowa	158.35	21.90	85.56
Missouri	149.79	16.33	65.28
North Dakota	192.80	21.51	67.84
South Dakota	249.34	25.45	89.15
Nebraska	274.93	33.61	107.89
Kansas	320.32	26.96	149.70
South Atlantic			
Delaware	222.59	23.39	96.00
Maryland	261.66	35.17	123.54
District of Columbia	283.42	50.36	153.49
Virginia	252.90	21.45	83.44
West Virginia	126.92	18.82	53.39
North Carolina	N/A	N/A	N/A
South Carolina	144.73	11.98	74.78
Georgia	212.76	16.16	99.37
Florida	159.46	14.16	61.35
East South Atlantic			
Kentucky	185.16	18.82	84.00

Table 3-1 (cont.)

	Disabled	AFDC Children	AFDC Adults
Tennessee	101.28	13.00	47.66
Alabama	N/A	N/A	N/A
Mississippi	77.82	4.43	N/A
West South Central			
Arkansas	80.59	9.24	33.32
Louisiana	109.38	14.63	56.21
Oklahoma	123.57	24.54	58.60
Texas	290.79	25.77	112.47
Mountain			
Montana	166.70	23.76	97.68
Idaho	199.09	17.11	107.84
Wyoming	166.77	16.03	67.20
Colorado	207.78	18.45	85.63
New Mexico	175.61	17.27	78.16
Arizona	N/A	N/A	N/A
Utah	196.28	14.98	59.99
Nevada	N/A	26.57	155.46
Pacific			
Washington	204.81	18.75	60.94
Oregon	170.50	9.58	57.64
California	462.62	29.79	116.14
Alaska	N/A	N/A	N/A
Hawaii	225.36	26.13	101.60

Source: Expenditures data are reported annually by the states to the National Center for Social Statistics. Summary statistics are published in *Numbers of Recipients and Amounts of Payments from Public Assistance Funds, 1970*. Estimates of eligibles were developed from various public assistance publications. The method of estimating eligibles is described in Appendix A.

We analyzed the impact of these and other variables on hospital utilization with the regression equations described below. Expenditures per eligible are divisible into two components: users per eligible (henceforth called USERS) and expenditures per user (henceforth called EXPENDITURES). The USERS variable serves as a proxy for hospital admissions. It is an imprecise proxy in that some users will have more than one admission during the year examined; regardless of the number of admissions, individuals are counted only once as users of inpatient services. The other dependent variable, EXPENDITURES, reflects various aspects of inpatient hospital service including length of stay, intensity of care, quality of service, and price. Each dependent variable is likely to be influenced differently by various regressors. Therefore, we estimate regressions for each component separately. The two equations estimated were the following:

$$\text{USERS}_{hj} = a_0 + a_1 \text{ DOCS}_j + a_2 \text{ BEDS}_j + a_3 \text{ PUB}_j + \qquad (3.1)$$
$$a_4 R^3 + a_5 \text{ INC}_j + a_6 \text{ SMSA}_j + a_7 \text{ NW}_j +$$
$$a_8 \text{ ED}_j + a_9 \text{ AGE}_j + a_{10} \text{ TURN}_j +$$
$$a_{11} \text{ SUP}_j + a_{12} \text{ TIME}$$

$$\text{EXPENDITURES}_{hj} = b_0 + b_1 \text{ DOCS}_j + b_2 \text{ BEDS}_j + \qquad (3.2)$$
$$b_3 \text{ PUB}_j + b_4 R^3_j + b_5 \text{ PRICES}_j +$$
$$b_6 \text{ INC}_j + b_7 \text{ SMSA}_j + b_8 \text{ NW}_j +$$
$$b_9 \text{ ED}_j + b_{10} \text{ AGE}_j + b_{11} \text{ TURN}_j +$$
$$b_{12} \text{ SUP}_j + b_{13} \text{ TIME}$$

where

USERS_j	= Ratio of users of hospital inpatient services to eligibles in state j
EXPENDITURES_{hj}	= Ratio of expenditures to users in state j
DOCS_j	= Ratio of physicians to population in state j
BEDS_j	= Ratio of hospital beds to population in state j
PUB_j	= Ratio of beds in state and local hospitals to all beds in state j
R^3_j	= A dummy variable equal to one in states using usual and customary fees and equal to zero in states employing fee schedules
INC_j	= Income per capita of eligible population in state j
ED_j	= Percentage of eligible population who are high school graduates in state j
NW_j	= Percentage of eligible population who are nonwhite in state j
SMSA_j	= Percentage of eligible population who live in SMSAs in state j
AGE_j (Disabled)	= Median age of disabled children in state j
AGE_j (Children)	= Percentage of eligible children under five years of age in state j
AGE_j (Adults)	= Percentage of eligible adult population who are females under thirty-five in state j
TURN_j	= Turnover rate in eligible population in state j

SUP_j	= Expenditures per eligible for optional services in state j
$PRICE_j$	= Average inpatient revenues per day in state j
TIME	= A dummy variable equal to zero in 1969 and one in 1970.

Equations (3.1) and (3.2) can be estimated with standard multiple regression methods. Multiple regression techniques not only provide tests of statistical significance, but also yield parameter estimates of relationships between dependent and independent variables when all other variables are held constant at their means. The parameter estimates (regression coefficients) can be easily translated into measures of elasticity, which can be defined as the percentage change in the dependent variable in response to a one percent change in the independent variable.[b] Though they remain highly useful statistics, elasticity estimates garnered from regression coefficients are technically valid only for small changes from the mean values of the dependent and independent variables. Furthermore, for valid inferences to be made from either regression coefficients or elasticities, it is necessary to assume that both variables included in the model and those which may have been excluded remain constant. Multiple regression methods also yield statistics on "goodness of fit" such as coefficients of determination (R^2), which indicate the percentage of variation in the dependent variable explained by the independent variables.

One statistical problem that plagued the study is multicolinearity. Multicolinearity exists when there is a high correlation between two or more independent variables. Its effect is to generate high standard errors on the coefficients of each of the correlated variables. As a result, T-values are lowered and it often cannot be determined whether the coefficient is significantly different from zero. Fortunately, the regression coefficients are not biased if correlated variables are not omitted from the regression. In the work we present in the following pages, there is a high degree of multicolinearity between medical price and physician availability, income and education, and between physician availability and the percentage of the eligible population living in SMSAs. The regression equations will include each of the correlated variables so that estimates of elasticities will be unbiased.

Hypotheses

Resource Availability

The ratio of hospital beds to population was used to test the hypothesis that increased bed availability or supply leads directly to increased bed utilization

---

[b]Elasticity estimates can be made directly if the variables are transformed into logs before estimating the regression.

rather than indirectly inducing an increase in demand through a fall in price. If this is a valid hypothesis, one would observe a positive relationship between the number of hospital beds per capita and the level of hospital admissions and length of stay, and thus with both hospital utilization variables.[c] As beds become scarce, more elective admissions are postponed or treated on an outpatient basis, and less serious cases are discharged sooner. The opposite, of course, should hold when an abundance of beds exists.

We hypothesized that the bed availability effect would be weaker where the ratio of public beds to all beds was high. The poor are much more likely than others to use state and local hospitals. However, state and local hospitals have less incentive than private hospitals to achieve budget surpluses or to minimize deficits. Thus they may be less likely to admit less serious cases and extend hospital stays unnecessarily in order to maintain high occupancy rates. Therefore, we hypothesize that the ratio of public beds to total beds will be negatively related to both utilization rates.

The number of physicians per capita was used to test the hypothesis that an abundance of physicians will result in greater use of hospital inpatient services. A relatively abundant supply of physicians is likely to lead to increases in the physician-induced demand for services or in the quality of service. Likewise, a shortage of physicians is likely to result in rationing or physician-induced decreases in the demand for services and/or in the quality of service. These effects may be muted somewhat by a substitution of ambulatory for inpatient care when physicians are relatively abundant and vice versa, greater use of hospitalization when a relative shortage exists.[d] In preliminary regressions (not shown in Table 3-3) the ratio of specialists to all physicians was used as an explanatory variable to test the hypothesis that specialists lead to greater utilization of hospital care. That is, where specialists are a relatively high proportion of available physicians, hospital care received by Medicaid eligibles would increase. We found no evidence for this hypothesis and the variable was dropped from the final regressions.

Prices and Reimbursement Arrangements

EXPENDITURES can vary across states because prices vary. We use price in the model to control for variations in prices across states. Prices should not have any

---

[c]The bed and physician availability variables are considered exogenous because Medicaid eligibles are a very small segment of the total demand for services. The demand by Medicaid eligibles for services and the prices set by state authorities can be assumed not to affect the availability measures.

[d]M.S. Feldstein [16] found that, for the U.S. population as a whole, the physicians per capita ratio was positively related to admissions. He argued that local physician availability may not only encourage the substitution of ambulatory for inhospital care but may also increase the total amount of care including inhospital care.

effect on the demand for services because the price to Medicaid users is zero. On the other hand, price may affect the quantity or quality of services per provider. Under ideal conditions an elasticity of EXPENDITURES with respect to price which is greater than one would suggest a positive supply response, while a price elasticity less than one would indicate a negative supply response to price. However, the prices used are average revenue per inpatient day in the hospital equations. Prices paid under Medicaid may differ from average hospital prices because of disproportionate numbers of unusual cases. They may also differ because of hospital reimbursement policies of the states.

Under Medicaid, as under Medicare, hospitals are reimbursed on the basis of their "reasonable costs." We assumed that the ratio of price per day paid by Medicaid to the average price per day for all inpatients was constant across states and, therefore, that analysis using average revenue per inpatient day would capture the influence of variation in Medicaid "reasonable costs."[e]

Precise data on reimbursement rates for physician services, such as the price allowed for an initial office visit, were not available. A set of dummy variables was used to represent the method of reimbursing physicians. The states were grouped into categories depending on their method of reimbursement. Thirty-eight states in 1969 and forty-six in 1970 had sufficient expenditure data for our purposes. Of these, nine states in 1969 and twelve in 1970 used usual and customary fees with maximums set by Medicare at the 75th percentile of prevailing charges in the locality for similar services. This method is generally regarded as the least restrictive. Ten states in 1969 and thirteen in 1970 used fee schedules based on the California Relative Value Schedule or other sets of fee schedules which essentially give the value of all procedures in terms of some standard procedure. The state then determines the price for the standard procedure and consequently determines all prices. Fee schedules give the physician little flexibility in setting fees and are generally regarded as the most restrictive form of reinbursement.

Nineteen states in 1969 and twenty-one in 1970 used usual and customary fees with maximums set below the Medicare levels. These states frequently use relative value studies to determine if physician's charges are excessive but the physician is free to set charges within the imposed limits. In general, this form of reimbursement is less restrictive than fee schedules but more restrictive than following medicare guidelines.[f] Table 3-2 provides information on reimbursement methods used by each state. It should be noted that many of the states with fee schedules have high physician population ratio and high average medical care prices.

---

[e]This assumption was based on discussions with staff members of the Medical Services Administration in HEW.

[f]There may be occasional overlap in restrictiveness between those states with fee schedules and those with low maximums on customary and usual fees. However, our results showed this variable to be consistently significant, which suggests that overlap was not a major problem. Nonetheless, estimates of effects of alternative methods are understated to the extent overlap exists.

Table 3-2
Methods of Physician Reimbursement, by State

Usual and Customary Fees (Maximum = Medicare)	Usual and Customary Fees (Maximum < Medicare)	Fee Schedules
Delaware	Arkansas (1970)	California
Florida (1970)	Idaho	Colorado
Georgia	Illinois	Connecticut
Indiana (1970)	Kentucky	District of Columbia
Iowa	Louisiana	Hawaii
Kansas	Maine	Maryland (1970)
Michigan	Missouri	Mississippi (1970)
Minnesota	Nebraska	New Jersey (1970)
Montana	Nevada	New York
South Dakota	New Hampshire	Oregon
Tennessee (1970)	New Mexico	Pennsylvania
Texas	North Dakota	Rhode Island
	Ohio	Utah
	Oklahoma	Washington
	South Carolina	
	Vermont	
	Virginia (1970)	
	West Virginia	
	Wisconsin	

States with 1970 in parentheses were used only in that year. Other states were used in both years.

The three arrangements outlined above were collapsed into two categories: fee schedules, and usual and customary charges (including states which do and do not follow the Medicare guidelines). The former is considered the more restrictive arrangement. The effect of reimbursement arrangements on USERS is not easy to predict. High reimbursement rates for physicians should increase the use of ambulatory care by increasing the willingness of physicians to participate. This could result either in better preventive care, thereby reducing hospitalization, or in discovery of more conditions requiring hospitalization. Similarly, high reimbursement, which leads to care by private physicians, probably increases access to private hospitals which have, in general, higher quality facilities and higher costs per day than state and local hospitals. Thus, higher physician reimbursement may also result in higher hospital EXPENDITURES.

Population Characteristics

The relationship between the incomes of the eligible populations and the use of medical services in general, and inpatient hospital services in particular, is difficult to predict. Ambulatory care utilization may be negatively correlated because individuals with higher income may be in better health due to the better housing and diet their income permits. In addition, for those individuals who have higher incomes due to employment rather than higher payment levels, obtaining medical care may entail a loss of earnings which would operate as a barrier to care. (Many low paying jobs do not provide paid sick leave.) On the other hand, higher income may positively affect utilization of health services by reducing the barrier imposed by additional costs of obtaining care such as transportation and child care. The use of ambulatory care may rise, but the effect of greater use of ambulatory care on hospital utilization is not clear. For example, use of ambulatory services may either substitute for hospital care by providing both preventive care and earlier treatment of acute conditions, or it may result in the more frequent discovery of conditions requiring hospitalization.

Place of residence (percentage of eligibles in SMSAs) is used to measure the affect of distance or accessibility on utilization of services. We hypothesized that persons not living in metropolitan areas would use fewer ambulatory services and, because they are less able to substitute outpatient for inpatient care, would have higher admission rates and shorter stays. In addition, the quality of care in rural hospitals is likely to be lower than that in urban hospitals. Thus we expected the hospital USERS ratio to be negatively correlated and the EXPENDITURES ratio positively correlated with the percentage of the eligible population living in SMSAs.

Education is another variable for which it is difficult to formulate an hypothesis. It may have a positive effect on USERS if more education is associated with greater physician contact which, in turn, leads to the discovery of conditions requiring hospitalization. Yet, it may also have a negative effect if it increases the use of preventive ambulatory care, or the effectiveness of self-care. There is no apparent reason to expect education to influence the EXPENDITURES variable.

A race variable was used to control for differences in utilization between whites and non-whites. One could hypothesize that differences in utilization could be due to racial discrimination by providers, or to lack of access to providers because they tend to locate in other neighborhoods. Lack of access to ambulatory facilities, in turn, might reduce the chance of discovering conditions requiring hospitalization. Similarly, we hypothesized that those non-whites who are hospitalized would receive fewer services and lower quality care, and therefore that EXPENDITURES would be lower in states with high proportions of non-whites in their populations.

An age variable was used to control for need in each regression. The median age of the disabled was used to control for health status differences. The greater the median age of the disabled population, the larger the need for hospital inpatient care. In addition, care needs will also be higher for states in which a high proportion of AFDC children and under five and a high proportion of adults are women under thirty-five.

Program Characteristics

The turnover variable was introduced to determine the degree to which state variations in inpatient hospital care utilization and expenditures are attributable to different ratios of part-year eligibles to full-year eligibles. If both groups of eligibles are in equal need of health care services per time period of eligibility, then the USERS and EXPENDITURES ratios in a given state should be lower the higher the ratio of part-year eligibles to total eligibles. On the other hand, if persons apply for assistance because of illness or disability, utilization rates per time period of eligibility should be higher, and the USERS and EXPENDITURES rate should approximate or perhaps exceed the full-year eligible experience. We hypothesized that the former effect would dominate and that the net result would be negative. Thus we expected the USER and EXPENDITURE ratios to be lower the higher the state's turnover rate.

A proxy variable to control for the support given the program by the state was also employed. States can control costs under Medicaid by provision of optional services to cash assistance groups, by provision of required and optional services to the medically needy, by its policies for reimbursement of providers, by bureaucratic controls or limits on utilization, and by provision of information to eligibles on their rights to as well as on availability of cooperative providers. The first two methods of control do not affect our analysis because hospital services are not optional and we consider utilization by only cash assistance groups. Reimbursement arrangements are employed as a separate variable. However the state can still exercise significant control by bureaucratic regulations or limits on excessive utilization such as by requiring authorization before admission of a Medicaid eligible to a hospital. It can also exercise control by the amount of information provided to eligibles on their right to care as well as on the availability and location of participating providers. The variable used was expenditures per eligible person on optional services. It is hypothesized that the more generous the state in support of services it is not required to provide, the greater its support of use of required services.

Data

Data on expenditures and users for all services, for all aid categories and for all states was provided by the National Center for Social Statistics (NCSS). States are required by law to report annual totals for expenditures and users. Summary statistics are then published in *Numbers of Recipients and Amounts of Payments Under Medicaid and Other Medical Programs Financed From Public Assistance Funds, 1969*. The published figures do not distinguish between recipients for whom money payments were authorized and those for whom they were not authorized. The first category consists of those who were receiving cash assistance. The second category includes the medically needy as well as those who are eligible for cash assistance but refuse it and those who are in institutions, such as homes for disabled, aged, etc. Because we were interested in only the first category, unpublished data was made available by NCSS. Users are an unduplicated count of persons with at least one contact for the individual service. Both expenditure and user data include persons eligible for any length of time up to one year.

The study was performed using pooled data from both 1969 and 1970. Some states (e.g., Tennessee, Massachusetts, Maryland, and Virginia in 1969, and Alabama, Massachusetts, and North Carolina in 1970) were excluded because of incomplete or inaccurate data. Some states were omitted for specific services either because the state did not have a program (e.g., Nevada has no cash assistance program for the disabled) or because the data appeared to be grossly in error (see Appendix C).

It was necessary to make estimates of eligibles in order to develop the USER ratios. NCSS does not have estimates of eligibles, nor is it clear how eligibility should be defined. Use of all persons below the poverty line would exclude all persons receiving cash assistance who are above the poverty line and include many below the line who would not be categorically eligible. Use of the unduplicated count of all recipients of one or more services would exclude all who used no services, which most likely varies widely across states. Our decision was to include as eligibles all those who were recipients of cash assistance at any time during the year. This would include as eligibles even those receiving assistance for one or two months. This definition, by including persons regardless of length of eligibility, is consistent with the definition of users.

Data on three population groups—the disabled (APTD), AFDC children, and AFDC adults—were used. The aged, though the largest users of Medicaid funds, were excluded because Medicare covered the bulk of payments (with the exception of nursing home care) for services used by Medicaid eligibles. Medicaid will pay for premiums, deductibles and coinsurance payments which Medicaid eligibles incur under the Medicare program. Thus, Medicaid expenditure data for the aged (for services also covered by Medicare) does not reflect the value of services rendered, but only those payments made by Medicaid. The blind were excluded because they account for less than one percent of Medicaid outlays. It should be emphasized that our interest is not specifically in the determinants of utilization by these groups as such, but in the explanatory variables which can be manipulated by public policy. A finding that a certain policy variable significantly affects utilization by one population but not by another is of principle interest to us not for the implications for the different groups, but because it weakens the argument that the variable can be used as an effective policy instrument.[1]

Results

The results of the disabled, AFDC children, and AFDC adult regression equations are presented in Table 3-3, respectively. Elasticity estimates for the more important variables are provided in Table 3-4. Each of the explanatory variables will be discussed in turn.

Hospital Bed Availability

Contrary to the findings of other research and our own hypotheses, the bed availability was not significant in any regression. The results may reflect the impact of the 1967 amendments to the Social Security Act which required that hospitals review admission and discharge decisions on a continual basis. In addition, several states employed limits on length of stay which, in general, call for case review after some period, say thirty or sixty days. Because limits affect only the tail of the distribution, it is difficult to tell how important they have been in practice. Because excessive stays are most likely to occur when the number of beds per capita is high, limits, if effective, would dampen the influence of the bed availability variable.

The absence of the expected association also suggests that the supply-creates-demand phenomenon may be less prevalent among hospitals which provide care for a large proportion of the poor. Relative to private hospitals, a higher percentage of the patients in public hospitals are poor. Occupancy rates in state and local hospitals in the United States in 1969 was 73.9 percent, which contrasts with an 80.8 percent occupancy rate in non-governmental non-profit hospitals [24]. There is perhaps less concern on the part of hospital administrators in state and local hospitals over budget deficits and, therefore, less incentive to maximize admissions and length of stay than in voluntary hospitals.

Public Hospital Beds

The ratio of public hospital beds to total beds (PUB) was negatively related to use of hospital inpatient care in the disabled and children USER equations, as expected. A 1.0 percent increase in the proportion of beds in public hospitals would be associated with a .06 percent decline in the USER ratio for the disabled and a .10 percent decline in the USER ratio for children. It was also negative and significant in the children EXPENDITURE equation, but insignificant in the other regressions. This provides some support for our hypothesis that states with a high proportion of public beds would have lower inpatient utilization rates.

Table 3-3
Hospital Inpatient Care Regression Results

	Constant	Beds	Pub	Docs	Price	R^3	Inc	Ed	SMSA	NW	Age	Turn	Sup	Time	$\bar{R}^2$
							USERS								
Disabled	36.22**	−.10	−.06*	−.23		2.21	−.01**	.52**	−.06*	.00	−.20	−.11	.03**	.52	.43
	(2.82)	(1.61)	(2.00)	(1.07)		(1.45)	(3.30)	(4.27)	(1.85)	(.06)	(.90)	(1.32)	(2.72)	(.62)	
Children	2.54	.03	−.03**	−.07		.15	+.01	−.00	−.01	−.04**	.35**	−.14**	.05*	.34	.53
	(1.01)	(1.14)	(2.35)	(.87)		(.24)	(.46)	(.09)	(1.38)	(3.50)	(4.18)	(4.91)	(2.04)	(.92)	
Adults	.27	.01	.01	.11		3.99**	−.02	.17	−.00	−.03	.26**	−.02	.05*	−1.09	.32
	(.50)	(.19)	(.52)	(.58)		(2.34)	(.25)	(.82)	(.06)	(1.31)	(3.14)	(.29)	(2.13)	(1.29)	
							EXPENDITURES								
Disabled	−858.32	−1.01	−1.01	67.93**	3.77	259.98**	5.50**	−13.79	4.23*	−.70	1.38	−1.87	1.01	53.07	.63
	(.91)	(.19)	(.47)	(3.38)	(.53)	(2.42)	(2.90)	(1.59)	(1.89)	(.30)	(.08)	(.32)	(1.53)	(.65)	
Children	−95.53	−.06	−.83*	18.44**	2.88*	78.92**	.97	1.82	.28	1.24**	−5.76	.23	.23	10.29	.70
	(.74)	(.04)	(1.64)	(4.00)	(1.76)	(3.04)	(.75)	(1.00)	(.58)	(2.88)	(1.62)	(.19)	(.20)	(.52)	
Adults	−126.77	−3.37	.39	22.32**	1.67	178.06**	6.06**	−1.52	1.97*	−.01	−1.67	−.44	−5.84	1.05	.57
	(.67)	(1.54)	(.48)	(3.15)	(.64)	(3.52)	(2.84)	(.46)	(2.14)	(.02)	(.69)	(.24)	(.19)	(1.46)	

Note: The first term on each line is the coefficient for each regressor. T-values are in parentheses; two asterisks indicate the variable is significant at the .05 level (one-tail test); one asterisk indicates the variable is significant at the .01 level.

Table 3-4
Selected Elasticity Estimates, Hospital Inpatient Care

	Beds	Pub	Docs	Inc	Race	SMSA
USERS						
Disabled	−.20	−.06*	−.11	−.04	.00	−.12*
AFDC Children	.20	−1.0**	−.11	.09	−.22**	−.11
AFDC Adults	.03	.02	.07	−.05	−.08	−.00
EXPENDITURES						
Disabled	−.04	−.02	.73**	.57**	−.02	.19*
AFDC Children	−.01	−.06*	.57**	.12	.14**	.04
AFDC Adults	−.27	.02	.48**	.54**	−.00	.21*

Note: Two asterisks indicate the variable is significant at the .05 level (one-tail test); one asterisk indicates the variable is significant at the .01 level.

Physicians Availability

The physician availability variable was not significant in the hospital USER equations, indicating that the distribution of physicians does not affect hospital admission of Medicaid eligibles. A relative abundance of physicians can result in a substitution of ambulatory care for inpatient care as well as an increase in the total amount of care. Insignificant results suggest that neither of the two effects are dominant. The physician availability variable was positive and significant at the .01 level in all EXPENDITURE equations. The results suggest that a 1.0 percent increase in the physician population ratio would lead, ceteris paribus to a .73 percent increase in EXPENDITURES for the disabled, and a .57 percent increase for AFDC children and a .48 percent increase for AFDC adults. The results probably reflect more intensive and higher quality inpatient care and perhaps longer hospital stays; the result is a higher average cost per user of inpatient services.

Physician Reimbursement

Our results provided no clear evidence that reimbursement arrangements for physicians affected the number of hospital users. The variable was positive in each USER regression but significant only in the adult USER equations. The coefficient in that equation indicates that customary and usual fee reimbursement accounted for a 5.0 percent higher USER ratio relative to fee schedule reimbursement. Reimbursement arrangements had a positive and statistically significant effect on the EXPENDITURES equation for all categories. The differences in average expenditures due to the alternative reimbursement arrangements were remarkably large. The results mean that states using the customary and usual fee method of reimbursement had higher average EX-PENDITURES by $260 for the disabled, $79 for children, and $178 for adults. The mean hospital inpatient EXPENDITURE in the two years were $1,038 for the disabled, $369 for children, and $533 for adults. The large impacts could have been due to higher quality care, use of more expensive hospitals, longer stays, and/or more services per stay.

Prices

The price variable was positive as expected but statistically significant only in the children EXPENDITURE equation. There was a high degree of multi-colinearity between hospital price and physicians per capita, which may explain the lack of significant results in the expenditure equations. The elasticities of expenditures with respect to price were either insignificant or less than one. Thus, given the problems of using a proxy variable for price and the existence of multicolinearity, the data provide no real evidence of a supply effect.

Income

The income variable was not significant in the inpatient USER equations. Income was positively related to use of physician and hospital outpatient services. Thus greater use of ambulatory services does not appear to affect hospital admissions or, vice versa, income barriers to ambulatory care do not result in greater hospital admissions. Income was positive in each EXPENDI-TURE regression and significant in the disabled and adult equations. This result probably reflects greater intensity or quality of care received by higher income individuals. In addition, greater use of physician services may increase access to private or voluntary hospitals which have higher costs per day.

Education

The results indicate that education does not play an important role in determining the use of hospital outpatient services. The variable was significant only in the disabled USER equation.

SMSA

The SMSA variable had the expected sign in the USER equations but was significant only in the disabled equation. The negative sign indicates that

Medicaid eligibles in rural areas are more likely to be admitted to hospitals. There was evidence of a positive effect on EXPENDITURES, probably reflecting the higher quality and cost of metropolitan area hospitals. In addition, urban residents, with fewer hospital admissions, may enter hospitals with more serious conditions on the average and thus have longer stays.

Race

The race variable was significant only in the children equations. The results indicate that non-white Medicaid children were less likely to use hospital care; the elasticity estimates suggest that a 1.0 percent increase in the percentage of eligible children who are non-white would reduce the percentage of eligible children using inpatient services by .22 percent. This result appears to follow from lower rates of utilization of physician and hospital outpatient services for non-whites. Lack of access to ambulatory care facilities appears to reduce the chance of discovering conditions requiring hospitalization. The race variable was positive and significant in the EXPENDITURE equation for children. This probably reflects the fact that with lower USER rates, those who are admitted to hospitals enter for more serious conditions and require more intensive care and longer stays.

Age

The age variable was positive as expected, reflecting the fact that children under five and women under thirty-five are more likely to enter the hospital. The variable was not significant in either disabled equation.

Turnover

We hypothesized that turnover rates would be negatively related to hospital utilization. The turnover rate was negative in each USER equation, but significant in only the children equation. The turnover rate should be negative if part-year and full-year eligibles are in equal need of hospital services per time period of eligibility. But, if a significant number of persons apply for assistance because of illness or disability, then USERS and/or EXPENDITURES should be higher per time period of eligibility. The effect of the turnover rate would be insignificant or perhaps positive. The insignificant effects suggest that the impact of persons applying for assistance because of illness or disability is strong enough to reduce the influence of the pure negative effect of normal periodic caseload turnover.

State Support

The state support variable was positive and significant in each USER equation. This suggests that states which are generous in their provision of optional services are also less likely to restrict access to hospital care. As a result, hospital admission rates are higher. The variable is not significant in the EXPENDITURE equations.

Summary

The principal conclusions of this chapter are:

1. Hospital bed availability does not affect use of hospital inpatient services by Medicaid eligibles, perhaps reflecting the effects of utilization review requirements.
2. Hospital bed utilization is lower in states where a high proportion of beds are in state and local hospitals. These hospitals appear to be less concerned with low occupancy rates so that the traditional theories of why bed supply affects utilization may not apply.
3. Physician availability strongly affects the level of expenditures per user of hospital services, perhaps reflecting the quality and intensity of care.
4. Physican reimbursement arrangements have strong effects on utilization of hospital inpatient care. Reimbursement through usual and customary charges results in higher levels of expenditures per user of inpatient care, probably due to increased quality and intensity of service. There was also some evidence that usual and customary charges result in higher hospital admission rates.
5. Non-white children are less likely than white children to use hospital inpatient services.
6. Children under five are more likely to be users of hospital inpatient services than other children. Likewise, women under thirty-five are more likely to use inpatient services than other adults.
7. The attitude of the state toward the program as reflected in the regulatory controls it is permitted to exercise apparently does affect the use of hospital services. States with more benevolent attitudes, as reflected in their expenditures on health care services they are not required to provide, have higher rates of hospital utilization.

Note

1. Data on physicians and physician specialists by state were obtained from the *Distribution of Physicians, Hospitals and Hospital Beds in the U.S., 1969,*

and the *Distribution of Physicians in the United States*, published by the American Medical Association. Data on hospital beds and hospital inpatient revenues per day by state were obtained from the guide issues of *Hospitals* published by the American Hospital Association in 1970 and 1971. Data on population characteristics for APTD Medicaid eligibles was taken from *Findings of the 1970 APDT Study—Part I: Demographic and Economic Characteristics* and *Part II: Financial Characteristics*, published by the National Center for Social Statistics. Data sources for population characteristics for AFDC recipients were the *Findings of the 1967 AFDC Study, Part I: Demographic and Program Characteristics and Part II: Financial Characteristics* and *Findings of the 1969 AFDC Study, Part I: Demographic and Program Characteristics and Part II: Financial Characteristics.* Both were published by the National Center for Social Statistics. Medical care prices were obtained from *Medicare and Medicaid: Problems, Issues, and Alternatives*, published by the U.S. Senate Committee on Finance. Information on methods of physician reimbursement was obtained from the Medical Services Administration. For further discussion of data sources see Appendix A.

4 Physician Services

Introduction

Physician services are provided to Medicaid eligibles by both office-based physicians and physicians in hospital outpatient care settings. Separate data are available for each provider group. Throughout this chapter, medical services will refer to services rendered in physicians offices. Medical services will also include services rendered by office-based physicians in hospital inpatient settings for which separate billings are made by those physicians. All independent laboratory and radiological services reported to Medicaid authorities in each state were also included with medical services. Services rendered by physicians and other professionals in hospital outpatient settings, (including laboratory and radiological services) for which billings are made by the hospital are included as outpatient services.

As shown in Table 4-1, expenditures per eligible person vary markedly across states for both medical services and outpatient services. Expenditures on medical services per eligible vary from over $170 in California to under $25 in Tennessee for the disabled, from over $35 in Vermont to under $2 in Louisiana for AFDC children, and from over $100 in Wisconsin to under $15 in Tennessee for AFDC adults. Expenditures per eligible for outpatient services vary from over $65 in New York to under $0.50 in Arkansas for the disabled, from almost $25 in New York to less than $0.25 in Arkansas for AFDC children, and from over $40 in New York to under $0.50 in Arkansas.

Several reasons can be given for the variations in expenditures on physician services among states. As discussed in Chapter 3, the availability of physicians varies widely among states. For example, the number of office-based physicians per 10,000 persons in 1970 ranged from 19.2 in the District of Columbia, 13.0 in California, and 12.3 in New York to 6.5 in South Carolina and 6.4 in Mississippi. The number of physicians available in hospital outpatient settings varies even more widely. The number of hospital-based physicians per 10,000 persons in 1970 varied from 11.5 in the District of Columbia and 7.4 in New York to .34 in Idaho and .29 in Montana. The generosity of schemes for reimbursing physicians, which encourages participation of office-based physicians and perhaps reduces the demand for services in hospital outpatient settings also differ among states (see Table 3-2 in Chapter 3).

Access to physician services is also affected by income, race, and place of residence. Families and individuals with low incomes may find costs of

51

Table 4-1

Physician and Hospital Outpatient Services, Expenditures Per Eligible, By State, 1970

	Medical Services			Hospital Outpatient Services		
	Disabled	Children	Adults	Disabled	Children	Adults
New England						
Maine	103.54	19.89	53.34	24.58	5.33	10.18
New Hampshire	86.21	16.09	58.19	8.27	3.00	8.42
Vermont	86.99	36.92	45.94	13.81	6.50	7.13
Massachusetts	N/A	N/A	N/A	N/A	N/A	N/A
Rhode Island	65.83	17.97	53.25	45.08	12.91	27.94
Connecticut	69.54	16.50	45.31	38.46	13.56	28.91
Middle Atlantic						
New York	47.60	16.45	44.77	66.93	24.53	43.65
New Jersey	67.08	16.10	25.29	29.96	7.93	12.24
Pennsylvania	37.16	10.14	27.17	N/A	N/A	N/A
East North Central						
Ohio	46.69	7.72	25.21	26.68	7.79	16.81
Indiana	63.70	12.16	50.36	15.32	3.10	8.55
Illinois	74.61	18.50	56.14	41.51	12.62	25.00
Michigan	114.67	17.61	66.30	23.79	5.30	10.17
Wisconsin	127.05	26.92	108.45	30.84	6.65	18.96
West North Central						
Minnesota	126.82	31.40	85.94	22.13	5.55	9.28
Iowa	96.08	24.10	72.24	11.57	3.74	9.25
Missouri	56.80	12.25	43.68	14.88	4.36	9.90
North Dakota	86.06	15.57	50.01	3.42	1.12	3.00
South Dakota	89.16	13.49	46.34	13.24	1.47	3.01
Nebraska	92.96	17.47	62.75	10.87	4.53	7.84
Kansas	114.96	22.44	86.81	14.86	5.03	10.88
South Atlantic						
Delaware	79.71	16.60	56.83	28.22	7.38	17.89
Maryland	36.68	6.63	21.04	60.74	16.05	36.36
District of Columbia	25.19	10.01	56.73	43.44	14.18	37.69
Virginia	69.96	15.32	46.82	34.50	7.80	20.25
West Virginia	53.00	14.24	35.23	6.30	2.44	4.39
North Carolina	N/A	N/A	N/A	N/A	N/A	N/A
South Carolina	72.06	10.09	48.93	7.70	1.91	6.04
Georgia	123.63	16.77	77.65	18.87	3.57	11.24
Florida	34.60	4.61	21.05	11.42	2.80	7.37

Table 4-1 (cont.)

	Medical Services			Hospital Outpatient Services		
	Disabled	Children	Adults	Disabled	Children	Adults
East South Central						
Kentucky	52.88	16.05	42.79	9.89	3.12	6.90
Tennessee	23.48	4.47	14.11	13.78	3.74	8.18
Alabama	N/A	N/A	N/A	N/A	N/A	N/A
Mississippi	33.14	5.15	N/A	2.72	.49	N/A
West South Central						
Arkansas	24.35	5.97	15.94	.36	.24	.28
Louisiana	25.00	1.66	14.40	4.53	1.27	3.56
Oklahoma	70.27	17.64	44.81	.51	.43	.32
Texas	151.47	19.47	78.55	17.20	4.01	9.41
Mountain						
Montana	104.78	19.54	73.79	10.12	2.09	4.81
Idaho	97.98	18.65	78.29	10.35	2.25	7.50
Wyoming	86.29	12.75	45.05	12.33	1.82	4.01
Colorado	84.82	14.01	53.19	21.83	3.74	8.16
New Mexico	73.81	13.48	49.53	7.82	1.73	4.65
Arizona	N/A	N/A	N/A	N/A	N/A	N/A
Utah	28.82	5.81	16.49	33.79	4.31	9.69
Nevada	N/A	17.83	95.68	N/A	4.89	17.09
Pacific						
Washington	62.14	13.85	34.38	15.28	2.75	4.79
Oregon	53.39	6.63	23.94	9.38	1.67	4.02
California	171.93	32.53	103.05	57.86	7.48	18.64
Alaska	N/A	N/A	N/A	N/A	N/A	N/A
Hawaii	88.82	24.70	54.70	63.46	11.63	26.23

Source: Expenditure data are reported annually by the states to the National Center for Social Statistics. Summary statistics appear in *Numbers of Recipients and Amounts of Payments under Medicaid: 1970*, published by the National Center for Social Statistics, Department of Health, Education, and Welfare. Estimates of eligibles were developed from various public assistance publications. The definition of eligibles includes anyone eligible during the year, which is consistent with the individuals for whom expenditures are reported (see Appendix A).

transportation and search for cooperative physicians serious deterrents to use of ambulatory care. Non-whites are widely believed to suffer from inadequate access to ambulatory care due to physicians preferences for locating in other neighborhoods as well as racial discrimination. Finally, persons living in rural areas have problems of access because of distance from either type of care setting. Persons living in metropolitan areas are much more likely than rural residents to use outpatient care because hospitals are more heavily concentrated in urban areas. As noted in Chapter 3, the incomes and racial and urban-rural compositions of eligible populations varies widely among states. Incomes range from over $65 per capita per month in Pennsylvania, New Jersey, Connecticut, Minnesota, and New York to under $30 in South Carolina and Arkansas. The percentage of the eligible population that is non-white ranges from under 5 percent in Vermont, Maine, and New Hampshire to over 80 percent in Louisiana, Florida, and Mississippi and nearly 100 percent in the District of Columbia. The percentage of the AFDC eligibles living in urban areas ranges from over 95 percent in New York, Rhode Island, and the District of Columbia to less than 15 percent in Vermont, North Dakota, South Dakota, and Mississippi.

We examined the impact of these and other variables on medical service and outpatient utilization with standard multiple regression techniques. The regression equations are described below. As in Chapter 3, expenditures per eligible for medical services and outpatient services are divisible into two components: users per eligible (USERS) and expenditures per user (EXPENDITURES). The USER variables indicates the percentage of eligible individuals who used the service at least once during the year. The EXPENDITURE variable reflects the effects of prices, quality of care, number of follow-up visits, and number of diagnostic and treatment procedures. The two medical services equations were as follows:

$$USERS_{mj} = c_0 + c_1\ ODOCS_j + c_2\ PRIM_j + c_3\ R3_j + c_4\ INC_j + (4.1)$$
$$c_5\ ED_j + c_6\ SMSA_j + c_7\ NW_j + c_8\ AGE_j +$$
$$c_9\ TURN_j + c_{10}\ SUP_j + c_{11}\ TIME$$

$$EXPENDITURES_{mj} = d_0 + d_1\ ODOCS_j + d_2\ PRIM_j + d_3\ R1_j + (4.2)$$
$$d_4\ R2_j + d_5\ PRICE_j + d_6\ INC_j + d_7\ ED_j +$$
$$d_8\ SMSA_j + d_9\ NW_j + d_{10}\ AGE_j +$$
$$d_{11}\ TURN_j + d_{12}\ SUP_j + d_{13}\ TIME$$

The two outpatient equations were the following:

$$USERS_{oj} = e_0 + e_1\ HDOCS_j + e_2\ INC_j + e_3\ ED_j + e_4\ SMSA_j + (4.3)$$
$$e_5\ NW_j + e_6\ AGE_j + e_7\ TURN_j + e_8\ SUP_j +$$
$$e_9\ TIME$$

$$\text{EXPENDITURES}_{oj} = f_0 + f_1 \text{ HDOCS}_j + f_2 \text{ INC}_j + f_3 \text{ ED}_j + \quad (4.4)$$
$$f_4 \text{ SMSA}_j + f_5 \text{ NW}_j + f_6 \text{ AGE}_j + f_7 \text{ TURN}_j +$$
$$f_8 \text{ SUP}_j + f_9 \text{ TIME}$$

The variables in the four equations are defined as follows:

USERS_{mj}	= Ratio of users of medical services to eligibles in state j
EXPENDITURES_{mj}	= Ratio of expenditures to users in state j
USERS_{oj}	= Ratio of users of outpatient services to eligibles in state j
EXPENDITURES_{oj}	= Ratio of expenditures to users in state j
ODOCS_j	= Ratio of office-based physicians to population in state j
PRIM_j	= Ratio of office-based primary care physicians to total office-based physicians in state j
HDOCS_j	= Ratio of hospital-based physicians to population in state j
$R1$	= States with usual and customary charges with maximum set at Medicare limits equal one; other methods equal zero
$R2$	= States with usual and customary charges with maximum set below Medicare limits equal one; other methods equal zero
$R3$	= States with usual and customary charges (the combination of $R1$ and $R2$) equal one; fee schedules equal zero
INC_j	= Income per capita of eligible population in state j
ED_j	= Percentage of eligible population who are high school graduates in state j
NW_j	= Percentage of eligible population who are non-white in state j
SMSA_j	= Percentage of eligible population who live in SMSAs in state j
AGE (Disabled)_j	= Median age of disabled population in state j

AGE (Children)$_j$ = Percentage of children under five years of age in state j

AGE (Adults)$_j$ = Percentage of adult population who are females under thirty-five in state j

TURN$_j$ = Turnover rate in eligible population in state j

SUP$_j$ = Expenditures per eligible on optional services in state j

PRICE$_j$ = Average medical services prices in state j

TIME   = A dummy variable equal to zero in 1969 and one in 1970

Hypotheses

Physician Availability

We hypothesized that the availability of office-based physicians as reflected in the number of office-based physicians per capita will affect the USER ratio for medical services in the following manner: in areas where office-based physicians are in short supply, Medicaid recipients may be denied services because of difficulty in obtaining appointments, lengthy queues, etc., and in areas where resources are in abundant supply, Medicaid recipients will be provided more adequate treatment. In either case, one would expect a positive relationship between physician availability and the USER ratio.

M. Feldstein has discussed the ability and willingness of the physicians to influence the demand for services in terms of availability [14]. He argues that because of the considerable consumer ignorance with respect to the appropriateness of medical services, the patient defers many utilization decisions to the physician. The physician acts as an agent for the patient in his decisions on appropriate service utilization, but because this agency relationship is incomplete (the physician's objectives do not always coincide with those of the patient) the physician's utilization recommendations will frequently result in a shift in the demand curve. Supply is typically thought of as affecting demand only through its influence on price. However, because the physician is able to shift the demand curve, the demand for services can be increased or decreased at constant prices. Feldstein argues that the propensity of physicians to shift the demand curve will depend on the relative availability of physicians. That is, an excess supply of physicians will lead to a provider-induced increase in demand rather than a fall in price. Likewise, an excess demand for physician services will call forth provider-induced reductions in demand rather than price increases.

Physician-induced demand shifts are more likely to occur with the EXPENDITURE variable. Thus, when physicians are relatively scarce, EXPENDITURES will be lower. Alternatively, EXPENDITURES will be high when physicians are relatively abundant because more thorough care will be provided as well as because of excessive services such as unnecessary follow-up visits, diagnostic and treatment procedures, and hospitalization.

The supply of hospital outpatient services, measured by the ratio of hospital-based physicians to total population, should influence demand for those services positively by reducing delays and, thus, time costs to patients. In addition, the presence of more physicians may increase the perceived quality of care, and thereby increase the demand for care. Thus, the USER ratio in the outpatient equations should be positively related to availability. The availability of physicians may also affect the EXPENDITURE ratio since hospital-based physicians can also influence the demand for services. However, hospital-based physicians are usually salaried and thus have no financial incentive to prescribe non-essential services; on the other hand, hospital outpatient departments are often used for teaching purposes which may encourage greater utilization of laboratory tests, X-ray facilities, and other services.

A second availability measure, the ratio of office-based primary care physicians to all office-based physicians, was used to test the hypothesis that the availability of primary care would increase use of medical services. The hypothesis is simply that the USER ratio for medical services will be higher, the higher the ratio of primary care physicians to total physicians. On the other hand, EXPENDITURES should be high when the ratio of primary care physicians to total physicians is low because a greater proportion of care will be provided by specialists. Care rendered by specialists is typically more sophisticated and expensive.

The specialty mix might also affect use of hospital outpatient services. Where the ratio of office-based primary care physicians to total physicians is low, the outpatient USER ratio may be high because a greater proportion of eligibles go to outpatient facilities for routine care. On the other hand, the ratio of office-based primary care physicians to total physicians may be positively related to the outpatient USER ratio if those primary care physicians refer a significant number of eligibles to hospital outpatient settings for specialists' services. This variable was not important in preliminary equations and the results were not included in Table 3-2. The insignificant results may reflect the offsetting effects of the two hypotheses set forth above.

Reimbursement Arrangements and Prices

The three alternative reimbursement arrangements outlined in Chapter 3 were analyzed to examine their impact on the utilization of medical services. In the medical services USER equations, both groups of customary and usual fee states were combined and compared with fee schedules. In the medical services EXPENDITURE equations, customary and usual fees with maximums at the 75th percentile of prevailing charges in the locality, as in Medicare, customary and usual fees with lower maximums and fee schedules were employed as separate dummy variables. Usual and customary fees with maximums at the 75th percentile of prevailing charges is generally regarded as the most generous form of reimbursement; fee schedules are regarded as the most restrictive. The price variable (average Medicare prices in each state), which was also included in the regressions, will capture much of the interstate variation in prices. Thus the reimbursement variable will reflect the deviation of state reimbursement rates from these average prices. It should again be noted that many of the wealthiest states employ fee schedules, the least generous form of reimbursement.

In general, it was hypothesized that restrictive reimbursement arrangements will result in lower USER and EXPENDITURE ratios. The USER ratio will fall if low reimbursement rates discourage physician participation, and as a result Medicaid eligibles either go without care or receive treatment in hospital outpatient departments. The EXPENDITURE ratio will be low if those physicians who do treat Medicaid patients limit the services they provide—if, for example, they perform less-complete diagnostic work, and fewer follow-up visits—as well as because the actual charges for physician services will be lower.

The utilization of hospital outpatient services may be influenced by the incentives provided by the states to office-based physicians to induce their participation. The methods of reimbursing office-based physicians were examined to test the hypothesis that more restrictive reimbursement arrangements are associated with an increase in the utilization of outpatient services. That is, the probability of using outpatient services increases as the incentives for office-based physicians to treat Medicaid eligibles diminish. Thus, the outpatient USER and possibly the outpatient EXPENDITURE ratio should be higher when fee schedules are employed.

We use prices in the medical services equations to control for differences in medical care price levels across states. Prices will not influence the demand for services because the cost to Medicaid recipients is zero, but may influence supply. With accurate price data, a price elasticity of expenditures greater than one would indicate a positive supply response to price, and a price elasticity less than one would mean a negative response. Unfortunately, the data available by state—average physician charges under Medicare—only approximate average prices under Medicaid because the elderly who receive Medicare services require different and more expensive kinds of mixes of medical procedures than disabled and AFDC Medicaid recipients, and therefore, Medicare prices will be uniformly higher.

In preliminary equations, the hospital outpatient price variable was also used as a control. However, it had a very low level of significance in all equations. Unfortunately, the variable used was based on state data on average revenue per outpatient visit, which may be an inadequate proxy for the prices paid under Medicaid.

Population Characteristics

Per capita income of the eligible population was used to test the sensitivity of utilization to income. Higher per capita income should result in increased utilization of both medical services and outpatient services, because income reduces the remaining economic barriers (for example, costs of transportation, day care, and search) to the use of these services. These influences should predominate despite the possibility that per capita income of the eligible population will be negatively related to utilization because (1) eligibles with higher income may be, on average, healthier due to factors such as better housing and diet, and (2) because working eligibles have higher foregone incomes.[a] Higher incomes may be associated with substitution of office-based physicians for care in outpatient settings. If this hypothesis is true, it should serve to reduce the income elasticities in the outpatient equations.

The effect of income on EXPENDITURES is less clear. Two opposing forces may serve to cancel one another. First, a positive impact of income on the USER ratio may reflect the provision of care to persons with less severe, and therefore, less expensive medical needs. If so, as income increases, EXPENDITURES should decrease. Second, income should affect EXPENDITURES in the same way it affects USERS—by reducing the burden of transportation and day care costs. If so, EXPENDITURES would increase with income.

Education is likely to have a mixed effect on the utilization of both medical services and outpatient services. On the one hand, education may be correlated with an appreciation of the value of medical care and with an understanding of how to obtain services, both of which would increase utilization. On the other hand, education may increase knowledge of preventive measures and methods of self-care (for example, how to substitute non-prescription drugs for a physician visit to treat a common cold). In the latter case, education would be negatively associated with both USER rates. If the former effect dominates in the USER ratios, the EXPENDITURE ratios may be negatively related to education because less-seriously ill eligibles will be users of services. Alternatively, if the latter effect dominates, EXPENDITURES might be positively associated with education as more serious cases, on average, receive treatment.

Location of residence was used to examine the effect of distance or accessibility on utilization of both medical and outpatient services. The greater the distance from suppliers of medical services, the lower utilization rates should be. Persons living in SMSAs are particularly likely to use hospital outpatient services more frequently because hospitals are more likely to be located in metropolitan areas and therefore are more accessible to them. However, since the measure used was the percentage of eligibles residing in an SMSA, rather than a direct measure of distance from suppliers, other factors may be captured in the variable. For example, SMSA residents may live in a more polluted environment or undergo greater tensions and therefore has greater health care needs than non-SMSA residents. In addition, preferences and attitudes toward medical services may be different in SMSAs and non-SMSAs, and this could lead

---

[a]In preliminary regressions, earned income of the mother was used to test for the effect of foregone earnings as a deterrent to utilization. It was never statistically significant, presumably because earnings are important only for a small minority of eligibles.

to differences in utilization rates. It is not clear which influences will dominate, although it seems reasonable to hypothesize that both the USER and EXPENDI-TURE variables for both medical and outpatient services will be positively related to urban residence.

A race variable was used to measure differences in medical and outpatient utilization between whites and non-whites. We hypothesized that non-white eligibles would be less likely to utilize medical services due either to racial discrimination by providers or to lack of access to providers because they tend to locate in other neighborhoods. This is more likely to affect the percentage of eligibles using services than the intensity or number of services received. Thus, the USER ratios are more likely to be affected than the EXPENDITURE ratios. We also anticipated a more marked differential between whites and non-whites in use of medical services than in use of outpatient services. Outpatient services are generally considered less desirable because the quality of care provided is allegedly inferior to that offered by physicians in private practice. There is a lack of personal and continuous contact with a physician, appointments are not normally available, and waiting time is longer. Thus, if non-whites have less access to medical services, they may substitute use of the less-preferred source, hospital outpatient care. If the substitution effect is strong enough to dominate the expected negative effect of race, the race variable will be positive in the outpatient USER equations.

Program Characteristics

We hypothesized that the turnover variable would be inversely related to both utilization variables for both services. As discussed in Chapter 3, the expenditure and user data do not distinguish between persons with full-year and those with part-year eligibility. Thus, it was necessary to introduce a variable to control for the effect of different ratios of part-year eligibles to total eligibles. If full-year and part-year eligibles are in equal need of health care services per time period of eligibility, then both USERS or EXPENDITURES in a given state should be lower, the greater the ratio of part-year eligibles to total eligibles. On the other hand, if persons apply for assistance because of illness or disability, utilization rates per time period of eligibility should be greater and the USER and EXPENDITURE ratios should be greater, the greater the ratio of part-year eligibles to total eligibles. We hypothesized that the former effect would dominate and that the net result would be negative in most cases. Turnover rates are highest in states with marked seasonal variations in employment, e.g., Washington, Oregon, California, Idaho, Montana, Vermont, and Colorado. This suggests that variance in the ratio of part-year to full-year eligibles is not due to variations because of illness, but to variation in persons entering because of seasonal fluctuations in employment. Thus, we expect USERS and EXPENDI-

TURES for both medical and outpatient services to be lower, the higher the state's turnover rate.

Expenditures per eligible person for optional services was used in each equation to control for the support given the program by the state. States can exercise considerable control on utilization through program regulations affecting the provision of care by physicians. States can also exercise control by the amount of information provided to eligibles on their right to care as well as on the availability and location of participating providers. The hypothesis is that the more generous the state in support of services it is not required to provide, the greater its support to use of required services. Because medical services are the more preferred mode of delivery for most individuals, state support may result in a substitution of medical services for outpatient care. However, we expect that the effect of state support on the total care provided will dominate any substitution effect.

Results

The hypotheses discussed above were tested in a set of regression equations using pooled data from 1969 and 1970. Equations for the Disabled, AFDC children, and AFDC adults were estimated separately. Sources for data used in the regression analysis are described in Chapter 3 and in Appendix A. The results for both services are shown in Tables 4-2 and 4-3. Estimates of elasticities for selected variables are shown in Table 4-4. The effects of each of the explanatory variables are discussed below.

Physician Availability

The results for the physician availability variable tended to conform to our expectations. However, in the medical services USER equations, the variable was either insignificant or negative. The unexpected results may reflect the fact that when office-based physicians are relatively abundant, hospital-based physicians are also in abundant supply and perhaps more conveniently located. In the hospital outpatient equations, hospital-based physician availability was positively related to USERS of that service, which supports the explanation of the greater accessibility of outpatient care. The variable was significant in both the AFDC children and AFDC adult equations. The elasticities were .18 and .15, respectively. The positive effects on the outpatient USER variable suggests that the availability effect operates on the number of recipients by increasing the demand for services through either reducing time costs to patients or by increasing the perceived quality of care available in outpatient settings.

In the medical services EXPENDITURE equations, the variable was consist-

Table 4-2
Physician Services Regression Results

	Constant	Docs	Prim	R1	R2	R3	Price	Inc
			USERS					
Disabled	34.38	−2.09*	47.84			−7.27*		.18**
	(1.00)	(−2.29)	(1.54)			(−1.93)		(2.64)
Children	−32.32	.07	62.76*			6.08*		.47**
	(1.31)	(.07)	(1.75)			(1.65)		(2.57)
Adults	13.09	−.37	59.04			.28		.51**
	.50	(−.42)	(1.44)			(.05)		(2.68)
			EXPENDITURES					
Disabled	−115.96	5.34*	52.00	68.96**	35.45**		10.46**	.03
	(.98)	(1.68)	(.50)	(5.30)	(2.62)		(2.46)	(.14)
Children	7.40	1.49	−9.40	13.22**	9.35**		2.42*	.07
	(.28)	(1.59)	(.26)	(3.33)	(2.52)		(1.94)	(.37)
Adults	−.36	4.09*	−78.55	64.81**	44.15**		2.07	−.16
	(.05)	(1.72)	(−.80)	(4.38)	(3.22)		(.53)	(.31)

ently positive and significant in the disabled and AFDC adult equations. The elasticities for the EXPENDITURE variable with respect to physician availability were .39, .33, and .40 for the Disabled, AFDC children, and AFDC adults, respectively. The results support the view that physicians can exercise significant control over the demand for services. Medicaid eligibles appear to receive more thorough care when physicians are relatively abundant; it is impossible to tell if the results reflect provision of excessive or unnecessary services.

The EXPENDITURE variable was not significant in the outpatient equations for any group. The results provide no evidence for physician-induced shifts in the demand for services in outpatient settings, presumably because of the different incentives facing hospital-based physicians.

Primary Care Physicians

The results indicated that the relative abundance of primary care physicians, when total physician availability is controlled for, is positively related to use of medical services. The elasticities of this variable with respect to the USER ratio for medical services were .42, .83, and .58 for the Disabled, AFDC children, and AFDC adults, respectively. This provides some evidence, although weak evidence

			USERS				
SMSA	NW	Ed	Age	Turn	Sup	Time	R^2
−.02	−.20**	−.07	.33	−.58**	.05**	1.28	.45
(−.23)	(−2.38)	(−.22)	(.58)	2.67	(2.40)	.58	
.02	−.15*	−.75**	1.58**	−.36*	.44**	−2.49	.39
(.31)	(−2.10)	(−3.16)	(3.00)	(−1.90)	(2.74)	(1.01)	
.03	−.19*	−.85**	.26	−.13	.14*	−1.81	.24
(.33)	(−2.21)	(−2.87)	(.98)	(−.70)	(2.02)	.67	

			EXPENDITURES				
−.78**	.25	2.97**	.44	−.29	.23**	−13.20*	.51
(3.34)	(.96)	(2.74)	(.24)	(−.41)	(3.04)	(−1.77)	
−.06	−.15	.68**	−.49	−.03	.11	−.54	.28
(−.94)	(.22)	(2.84)	(−.99)	(−.18)	(.71)	(−.23)	
−.02	.14	1.23	.08	.30	.22	−5.35	.31
(.10)	(.67)	(1.52)	(.12)	(.63)	(1.19)	(.76)	

Note: The first term on each line is the coefficient for each regressor. T-values are in parentheses; two asterisks indicate the variable is significant at the .05 level (one-tail test); one asterisk indicates the variable is significant at the .01 level.

in view of the fact that only one variable achieved statistical significance, that altering the specialty composition of the supply of physicians would result in greater use of medical services by the poor. We found no evidence that a relative scarcity of office-based primary care physicians increased use of hospital outpatient services.

Reimbursement Arrangements

There was no consistent evidence of a positive relationship between reimbursement arrangements and the USER ratio. The reimbursement variable was significant and negative in the disabled equation and significant and positive in the children equation. On the other hand, the reimbursement variable was positive and significant at the .01 level in the EXPENDITURE equations for all three groups. The difference in the effect on the two utilization measures was probably due to the fact that the USER ratio largely reflects patient decisions, while the EXPENDITURE ratio is controlled by physicians.

The results in the EXPENDITURE equations suggests that fee schedules reduce expenditures on physician services per user; (1) by $68.96 for the disabled, $13.22 for AFDC children, and $64.81 for AFDC adults, relative to

Table 4-3
Hospital Outpatient Services Regression Results

	Constant	HDOC	Inc	Ed	SMSA	NW	Age	Turn	Sup	Time	$\bar{R}^2$
USERS											
Disabled	20.22	.77	.08*	-.06	.24**	-.05	-.11	-.26*	-.03*	2.60*	.56
	(.91)	(1.29)	(1.68)	(.31)	(5.22)	(1.02)	(.27)	(1.75)	(1.89)	(1.66)	
Children	-7.46	1.23**	.32**	-.49**	.08**	-.01	.61*	-.11	.15*	-.75	.67
	(1.42)	(3.07)	(3.45)	(4.10)	(2.81)	(.28)	(2.40)	(1.14)	(1.82)	(.62)	
Adults	-3.51	1.52*	.32*	-.73**	.13**	-.03	.31	.14	.08*	-2.96	.48
	(.38)	(2.29)	(2.19)	(3.13)	(2.58)	(.52)	(1.62)	(.94)	(1.55)	(1.42)	
EXPENDITURES											
Disabled	137.35	-1.65	.42**	.43	.45**	.46**	-3.07*	-.09	.13**	9.98*	.55
	(1.80)	(.83)	(2.50)	(.63)	(2.92)	(2.50)	(2.23)	(.18)	(2.42)	(1.87)	
Children	-7.18	.56	.19*	-.31*	.18**	-.02	.58*	.01	.32**	3.79**	.66
	(1.06)	(1.12)	(1.71)	(2.15)	(4.80)	(.54)	(1.78)	(.12)	(3.18)	(2.57)	
Adults	-11.93	.93	.47**	-.59*	.23**	.05	.35	.10	.05	1.52	.51
	(1.04)	(1.07)	(2.43)	(1.96)	(3.44)	(.65)	(1.42)	(.57)	(.85)	(.56)	

Note: The first term on each line is the coefficient for each regressor. T-values are in parentheses; two asterisks indicate the variable is significant at the .05 level (one-tail test); one asterisk indicates the variable is significant at the .01 level.

Table 4-4
Selected Elasticity Estimates, Medical and Hospital Outpatient Services

	Docs	Prim	Inc	Race	SMSA
USERS		Medical Services			
Disabled	−.30*	.42	.31**	−.08**	−.01
AFDC Children	.01	.83*	.56**	-.14*	.03
AFDC Adults	−.06	.58	.46**	−.15*	.03
EXPENDITURES					
Disabled	.39*	.23	.03	.05	−.31**
AFDC Children	.33	−.13	−.08	−.02	−.08
AFDC Adults	.40*	−.45	−.09	.06	−.01
		Outpatient Services			
USERS					
Disabled	.07	−	.33*	−.05	.42**
AFDC Children	.18**	−	.87**	−.02	.27**
AFDC Adults	.15*	−	.58*	−.05	.28**
EXPENDITURES					
Disabled	−.07	−	.71**	.18**	.34**
AFDC Children	.05	−	.35*	−.03	.37**
AFDC Adults	.06	−	.58**	.05	.34**

Note: One asterisk indicates the variable is significant at the .05 level (one-tail test); two asterisks indicate the variable is significant at the .01 level.

customary and usual charges with maximum charges at the 75th percentile and (2) by \$35.45 for the disabled, \$9.35 for AFDC children, and \$44.15 for AFDC adults relative to customary and usual charges with lower maximums. Mean expenditures on physician services per user were \$120.47 for the disabled, \$39.59 for AFDC children, and \$92.12 for AFDC adults.

A basic issue is whether the effect of the reimbursement variable on EXPENDITURES is too large to be merely a price effect, that is, to effect only a differential in fees paid physicians, or if the quantity of services delivered is affected. An estimate of the average quantity of services per user can be derived by dividing the mean expenditure by the mean price for each category of recipient. Dividing these quantity estimates into the appropriate coefficient yields estimates of the differences in fees charged, if there is no quantity effect due to the alternative reimbursement arrangements. Because the mean Medicare price will be roughly equivalent to R_1, the quantity estimates will be minimum estimates and the fee differentials will be the maximum differentials. If the fee differences appear large relative to average prices, then there is reason to believe reimbursement procedures have, in fact, also affected the average quantity of services per user. We observed the differentials shown in Table 4-5.

In Table 4-5, the base is the average price in states utilizing the fee schedule reimbursement method. The dollar values shown are the price differentials relative to fee schedules for states using customary and usual fees with maximum charges set at the 75th percentile (R_1), for states using customary and usual fees with maximum charges set below the 75th percentile (R_2), and for the mean price in all states. For example, under customary and usual fees with maximums at the 75th percentile, prices for services rendered the disabled are at the most $4.69 higher than under a fee schedule arrangement. The ratios of the price differential to mean price are also provided in Table 4-5. The differentials relative to mean prices appear moderate, suggesting that little of the differential is attributable to changes in the quantity of service delivered.

The effect of low reimbursement rates such as fee schedules on the number of services supplied depends on physician responses [23]. If rationing or physician-induced reductions in demand for services are the most common response, quantity supplied would fall. If physicians increase the efficiency of their operations, quantity supplied would increase. If service quality were reduced, increases in quantity supplied would most likely be observed, but the direction of change would depend on the elasticities of both supply and demand with respect to quality. Our regression results do little to clear up this ambiguity. We observe little increase or decrease in quantity supplied and have no way of discerning changes in quality. The results do suggest that no effect is dominant, with the possible exception of the quality effect. They also strongly indicate that fee schedules have very marked effects on expenditures per user of physician services. As a result, health care financing programs could obtain significant savings in costs under such programs as Medicaid by employing fee schedules. However, such programs would incur the risk of adverse effects on quality of services rendered their clients. The magnitude of this risk is unknown.

Table 4-5
Price Differentials Under Alternative Reimbursement Arrangements, Assuming No Supply Effects

	Disabled		AFDC Children		AFDC Adults	
		% of Mean		% of Mean		% of Mean
	Differential	Price	Differential	Price	Differential	Price
R_1	$4.69	57.2	$2.73	33.4	$5.82	70.4
R_2	2.41	29.4	1.93	23.6	3.96	47.9
Mean Price	8.20		8.20		8.20	

The reimbursement variable was used in preliminary outpatient service equations. The variable was not significant in any USER or EXPENDITURE equation, thus providing no evidence that restrictive reimbursement arrangements result in a substitution of hospital outpatient services for physician services. Even if fee schedules result in the provision of fewer medical services, it does not appear to cause an increase in hospital outpatient care in compensation.

Prices

The price variable was significant in only the disabled and AFDC children EXPENDITURE equations. However, the variable was positive as expected in all equations. The low level of significance may be due to high correlations between the price and physician availability variables.

Income

The income variable was positive and significant in the USER equations for both the medical services and outpatient care equations. The income elasticities in the medical services equations were .31 for the disabled, .56 for AFDC children, and .46 for AFDC adults. In the outpatient service equations, the elasticities were .33 for the disabled, .87 for AFDC children, and .58 for AFDC adults. The results clearly indicate that the probability of using either service increases with income. As income increases, the burden of transportation, day care, and other costs decrease. The income elasticities were highest for children and lowest for the disabled, perhaps because many valuable services for children are preventive and thus in some sense optional or discretionary. If income is high, more of these services are used and, vice versa, if income is low, many services for children are postponed or never obtained. For the disabled, greater hardship is associated with failure to use services and thus utilization is less responsive to changed in income.

Income elasticities are difficult to measure adequately. First, our income elasticities may have been overstated because of a correlation between the level of per capita income of the eligible population and the probability that information on eligibility for and availability of services will be provided. If such information and income are highly correlated, then the income elasticities are overstated. However, expenditure per eligible on optional services was used to control for the effects of the attitude and generosity of the state. Thus we believe the income elasticities basically reflect the responsiveness of the poor to changes in income. Second, there may be cultural differences between Medicaid eligibles in high income and low income states. We attempted to control for such differences with race, education and urban-rural composition variables. If cultural differences remain, then income elasticities are overstated and raising incomes in low income states will have less than the estimated effects on use of physicians services.

The income variable was insignificant in the medical services EXPENDITURE equations but significant and positive in the outpatient EXPENDITURE equations. The positive effect in the outpatient equations suggests that income affects EXPENDITURES in the same way it affects USERS—by reducing the burden of transportation, day care, and other costs of using medical services. The insignificant effects of income in the medical services equations suggest that this positive effect may be offset by a decline in the average seriousness of cases as the USER rate increases, thus reducing EXPENDITURES.

Education

The education variable was negative in the medical services and outpatient USER equations. It was not significant in the disabled equations for either service but was significant at the .01 level for both AFDC children and adults for both services. The findings support the hypothesis that education leads to substitution of self-care, increased use of preventive measures, and elimination of unnecessary ambulatory services. The insignificant effects for the disabled may reflect the fact that the disabled are largely a chronically ill group and substitution of self-care and general preventive care would necessarily be less important. The education variable was positive in the medical services EXPENDITURE regressions and significant for the disabled and AFDC children. This supports the view that when preventive measures and self-care are substituted for physician services, the decreased number of individuals who do visit physicians have more serious conditions which are more expensive to treat. However, the education variable was negative and significant in two outpatient EXPENDITURE equations. This is contrary to expectations and may reflect the same influences that were observed to operate on the education variable in the outpatient USER equations.

SMSA

The SMSA variable was insignificant in all but one medical services equation. The exception was the disabled EXPENDITURE equation where the results indicate that the rural disabled who use medical services receive more intensive care than their urban counterpart. We hypothesized that persons living in SMSAs use hospital outpatient services more frequently because hospitals are more likely to be located in SMSAs. We found consistent evidence that SMSA residence positively affects both utilization variables; the variable was statistically significant in all equations for both years. In the USER equations, the estimated elasticities ranged from .27 to .42, meaning that a 1.0 percent increase in the proportion of Medicaid eligibles living in SMSAs resulted, ceteris paribus, in a .27 percent to .42 percent increase in the USER ratio, depending on eligibility category. In the EXPENDITURE equations, the estimated elasticities varied from .34 to .37. These differences in the utilization of ambulatory services do not appear to result from substitution of hospital outpatient care for medical services, for the SMSA variable indicates no difference in the latter by SMSA and non-SMSA residents. Since there is no greater use of outpatient services and no difference in use of medical services, it appears that SMSA residents receive more ambulatory care than Medicaid eligibles living in rural areas. Thus distance and accessibility do affect utilization, unless location of residence is associated with significant differences in either attitudes toward medical care, or the need for medical services.

Race

The race variable indicated that non-whites were less likely to be users of medical services. The variable was significant and negative for each group. The results indicated that a 1.0 percent increase in the percentage of non-whites in the eligible population would result in a decrease of .08 percent in the disabled USER ratio, .14 percent in the AFDC children USER ratio, and .15 percent in the AFDC adult USER ratio. Thus it appears that barriers to use of medical services by blacks exist despite provision of care at zero price. The race variable was not significant in the EXPENDITURE equations, suggesting no variation in intensity of care once non-whites gain access to office based providers. The race variable was not significant in the outpatient equations, with the exception of the disabled EXPENDITURE equation. Thus there is no apparent difference between whites and non-whites in use of outpatient services. Yet because there is a significant difference in the use of medical services and no difference in use of outpatient services, it is clear that non-white Medicaid eligibles have less access to services of physicians even with control for income, education, and other variables.

Age

The age variable results showed that children under five were more likely to use both medical and hospital outpatient services.

Turnover

It was hypothesized that the turnover variable would be inversely related to both utilization variables. The variable was negative and significant in the disabled equations for both services and in medical services equations for AFDC children. The lack of significant findings in the remaining equations indicates that, in general, the effect of persons applying for assistance because of illness or disability appears to be influential enough to reduce the strength of the pure negative effect of unemployment induced turnover.

State Support

The state support variable was positive and significant in most equations. This suggests again that states which are generous in their provision of optional services are more likely to provide information to eligibles and less likely to place limitations on service delivery by physicians. As a result, the percentage of eligibles using services as well as the level of outlays per user are higher.

Summary

The principal conclusions of this chapter are as follows:

1. The availability of physicians in office-based settings strongly and positively effects the level of expenditures per user of medical services, thus supporting the view that physicians can control the level of demand for their services. A 1 percent differential in the physician-population ratio was associated with a .33 percent to .40 percent differential in expenditures per user.
2. The availability of physicians in outpatient settings significantly effects the percentage of eligibles using those services. It does not appear to affect the level of expenditures per user, perhaps because of the different incentives facing hospital based physicians.
3. An increase in the relative availability of primary care physicians, vis-à-vis specifalists would appear to increase the percentage of eligibles using medical services in office-based settings.
4. The level of expenditures per user of physician services was strongly related to the generosity of reimbursement. The quantity of services supplied did not appear to be largely affected. The effect on quality of services provided could not be determined. It appears that Medicaid could obtain significant reductions in costs by employing fee schedules, but only by taking risks (the magnitude of which are uncertain) of reducing the quality of care to its clients.
5. Medicaid eligibles appear to be quite responsive in their use of both medical services and outpatient services to changes in income. The income elasticities were particularly high for children.
6. Families and individuals living in urban areas are more likely to use physician

services. There was no difference in use of medical services but significantly greater use by SMSA residents of services rendered in outpatient settings.

7. Non-white Medicaid eligibles have less access than their white counterparts to services of physicians even when care is free and income, education, and other factors are controlled for. There was a significant difference in use of medical services, but no difference in use of outpatient services.

8. States with relatively favorable attitudes toward the program, as reflected in the generosity of their provision of optional services, have higher rates of utilization of both medical services and outpatient care. This reflects provision of information to eligibles on rights to and availability of care as well as the degree of regulatory control over service delivery by physicians.

5 Alternatives to Medicaid

Changing the Structure of Medicaid

In Chapter 2, we examined the coverage by Medicaid of the health service needs of the poverty population. We found that there are great differences among states in the number of poor covered and in benefits provided. Some states cover male-headed families if the family head is unemployed, while others do not. Some states provide basic coverage to the near poor while others provide none. Some provide several optional benefits such as prescription drugs and dental care while others provide only the required services. Finally, the level of income families or individuals can have and remain eligible varies enormously among states. As a result we found that states such as Arkansas, Texas, and Mississippi covered less than 10 percent of the population falling within the Census definition of poverty, while states such as New York, California, and Pennsylvania appear to cover most of the poor and many of the near poor. We made estimates of the average value of benefits to eligibles in 1970 and found they varied from approximately $100 in Arkansas to over $900 in New York for the disabled and from approximately $10 in Mississippi to over $110 in Vermont for AFDC children for services which states were required to provide. The value of optional services varied from around $3 per person in Idaho to almost $300 in California for the disabled and from under $1 in Louisiana to over $40 in New York for AFDC children.

Such inequities follow from the federal state cost sharing feature of the program. The federal government sets minimum standards in terms of population coverage and a benefit package and offers to participate in the costs of the program. It offers to share 50 percent of costs in wealthy states such as New York and California and up to 83 percent of costs in a state such as Mississippi. The federal government also offers to participate in the bearing of costs if the state wishes to provide optional benefits to the covered population and basic and/or optional services to the medically needy. The result has apparently been that 50 percent cost sharing provides sufficient incentive for wealthy states to provide generous benefits to large numbers of poor and near poor while 70 to 80 percent cost sharing is not sufficient to induce poor states to provide more than the basic benefit package to a small component of the poverty population.

In thinking about alternatives, it is useful to consider the rationale behind government involvement in health care financing. The government assists families and individuals in paying for health care for essentially two reasons.

73

First, hospital, medical, and other health related expenses are often unpredictable and large in relation to income. Because of inadequate information, the uneven distribution of income, and the unwillingness of insurance firms to incur very large risks, the private market has failed to provide insurance against catastrophic illness. This argument, of course, justifies provision of assistance to families at any income level who happen to incur expenses large in relation to income. Second, some groups use less health care than the rest of the population would like them to be using. For example, parents particularly among the poor are often not good agents or representatives for the interests of their children. The result is that poor children often do not use necessary preventative or remedial services. Thus, it may be in society's interest to provide services to children at low costs to encourage higher levels of utilization. Furthermore, health can be viewed as an investment in human capital; that is, better health leads to a more productive labor force, which in turn means a more productive national economy. Consequently, it is in the interest of society that its members maintain good health, justifying provision of health services at less than market prices for those likely to "underspend" on health services.[a] Finally, altruism or humanitarianism suggests that the welfare of all society will be increased if the health of the poor is increased.

The fact that the poor may not consume health services in amounts deemed appropriate by the rest of society suggests that health services should be provided at less than market prices. It does not necessarily suggest all services should be provided at zero price, as under the present structure of the Medicaid program. Routine, predictable medical care is no more urgent or crucial than food or housing, which are not currently provided to the poor at zero cost. When available funds are limited, it is difficult to justify subsidies for health services which exceed those provided for food or housing.

Given this rationale for government involvement in health care financing, it follows that any such program should adhere to basic principles of equity and allocative efficiency. First, the program should seek to treat persons in identical circumstances in a similar fashion. Second, it should allocate scarce funds among those poor who need it most and among services which are most important and most likely to result in severe hardship if not subsidized.

As discussed above, the Medicaid program meets neither of these objectives. The principles of equity and allocative efficiency are more likely to be implemented under a program which meets the following objectives:

---

[a]At least three arguments may be made for the view that an underinvestment in one's own health would occur without subsidization. First, the capital market for investment in human beings is imperfect because of the difficulty of protecting against the risk of default. Second, in imperfectly competitive markets, workers are paid less than the value of their marginal product; thus, part of the benefits from their investment in human capital accrue to others than themselves. Third, where paid sick leave exists, the cost of absenteeism resulting from illness is borne by the firm, not the workers.

1. The program should provide for universal population coverage with benefit packages which are uniform across income groups. Single individuals, childless couples and male-headed families should be accorded treatment similar to others of equal income status. Poor families and individuals living in less wealthy states should have financial access to the same package of services as similar groups in wealthy states.
2. Cost sharing provisions should be limited so that the burden placed on the poor and near poor is not high in relation to income. Yet they should not be so low that there are inadequate incentives to use services efficiently. We assume that unnecessarily expensive programs which would reduce funds available for other valuable purposes are undesirable. Cost sharing provisions for the poor should also be integrated with the provisions for middle income families so that serious "notch" effects do not occur.
3. Reimbursement arrangements should encourage efficiency and control costs. However, reimbursement schemes should not give incentives to providers to treat the poor and non-poor differently.
4. Programs should not be so complex that their provisions are beyond the understanding of the poor. The program should be designed so that efficient administration is feasible; the poor are more likely than the non-poor to be adversely affected by inefficient administration.
5. The program should be financed in a manner which will not place severe burdens on the poor or near poor. It is also important that the poor not be discouraged from seeking employment because of significant increases in taxes or premium contributions. Firms should not be provided with incentives to hire part time rather than full time workers in order to avoid health insurance contributions or to hire "low risk" individuals rather than "high risk" individuals to minimize health insurance costs.

The next section will analyze the impact four national health insurance plans would have on the delivery of care to the poor. Before beginning that discussion, the issue of cost sharing merits greater attention. It was argued above that while population coverage should be universal, it is not necessary or desirable that services be provided at no cost. Several writers, most notably Martin Feldstein [17] and Mark Pauly [33], have argued that a system of deductible, coinsurance, and limits which vary with income would assure an equitable and efficient system of subsidization. It is argued that cost sharing which varies with income can serve to insure that scarce funds are allocated to those most in need and among the most valuable services. Government assistance to families or individuals would decline as income levels increase, but would increase as health care expenses increased. The deductible and coinsurance liabilities would discourage use of unnecessary services while encouraging search for more efficient low cost producers.[1] Cost sharing would make it feasible to finance a broader benefit package, including items such as dental care which are post-ponable for many but impose severe hardship on others. Cost sharing may also make the system easier to "police" by making it more difficult for providers to collect for services not rendered.

It should be noted that there is widespread disagreement on the efficiency of cost sharing. Many writers argue that deductibles and coinsurance perform the allocation function in an inefficient manner. That is, patients have insufficient knowledge to make rational calculations of the benefits and costs of their choices, while physicians and other providers, who presumably do possess adequate information, are only indirectly affected by the prices facing consumers. These critics stress that other forms of cost control be imposed, particularly those which impinge on the physician. It is also argued that if cost sharing is employed to reduce the impact of the program on the federal budget, this objective could be equally well achieved through income related premiums. This approach would avoid the necessity of imposing financial burdens on the sick at time of illness. It is difficult to assess these arguments because of the paucity of real evidence on the actual effect of cost sharing on the types of decisions made by patients. However, in the remainder of this chapter we assume that with the extent of current political pressure to limit the level of governmental outlays, equitable cost sharing provisions for the purpose of limiting the impact on both total and federal costs are desirable. That is, a national health insurance program which would increase the financial access of the poor to health services, provide coverage against the catastrophic financial burdens of illness, and control costs could become law with less of a burden on the federal budget if cost sharing provisions were included than if they were not.

Ideally, income maintenance reform would precede or accompany reform of health care financing programs. Routine predictable medical expenses can be considered the province of general income maintenance, in the same manner as food, housing and other essentials. Income maintenance reform should include coverage of the many poor who are presently excluded and incorporate a minimum level of income transfers sufficient to cover routine medical expenses in addition to other items deemed appropriate. Because many people, particularly those who remain at lower levels of the income distribution, may spend less on health services than is socially desirable, medical care should still be provided at less than market prices. Under such an arrangement, income maintenance payments should be set at levels which include, at a minimum, the average value of the family or individual's liability. Limits on the liability of a family or individual, set as a percentage of income, would insure against catastrophic expenses.

If income maintenance reforms do not occur, deductibles and coinsurance would impose severe hardships on persons living in states with stringent public assistance programs. In the absence of income maintenance reform, the gains in efficiency which would come about through coinsurance and deductibles should be sacrificed in the interests of equity. That is, cost sharing levels should be very low or non-existent for very low income individuals and increase with income at rates which will maintain equity and avoid adverse work incentives.

One difficulty with a plan in which deductibles and coinsurance vary with income is that the implicit marginal tax rate on income becomes rather high, perhaps exceeding 100 percent. Under the current structure of public programs for the poor, low income families face the loss of a certain percentage of income maintenance payments (67 percent following an initial earnings disregard and other deductions), higher costs for food stamps, social security taxes, and reduced housing subsidies as earnings increase. Medical care outlays which also increase with income would further increase the marginal tax rate and further augment the work disincentive features of public assistance programs.

All major national health insurance plans before Congress would replace Medicaid. However despite many common features which markedly improve their coverage, there are significant differences in the effects different plans would have on the poor. This can be illustrated by examining the plans likely to be given the most serious consideration in the Congress: the Nixon Administration, Kennedy-Griffiths, Kennedy-Mills, and Long-Ribicoff proposals. We make no effort to provide a comprehensive analysis of all issues raised by the plans, but focus on issues affecting financing and delivery of care to the poor.[2] That is, we consider each of the plans in light of the objectives we have developed above. Critical issues not discussed include provisions for protection against catastrophic expenses for individuals and families of all income levels, cost control mechanisms other than cost sharing and physician reimbursement arrangements. the role of the federal vs. state governments, and the role of private insurance firms. We also do not attempt to rank the plans in terms of acceptability but rather focus on significant problems which need careful legislative consideration.

Four Alternative Plans

The Comprehensive Health Insurance Plan (CHIP)

The Nixon Administration's plan (CHIP) has three components: a plan for employed persons, called the Employee Health Care Insurance Plan (EHIP), a restructured Medicare program for the aged, termed the Federal Health Care Insurance Plan (FHIP), and a plan for low income and high risk individuals and families, the Assisted Health Care Insurance Plan (AHIP). We will be concerned primarily with the latter. AHIP is designed primarily to provide coverage for all families below $5,000 income, all individuals below $3,500, and non-working and very high risk working families between $5,000 and $7,500 income ($3,500-$5,250 for individuals). All other families and individuals could elect to choose coverage under AHCIP by paying the required premium. Services covered under the plan include hospital services, physician services, prescription drugs, inpatient mental health services (thirty full or sixty partial days), outpatient mental health services (thirty visits to a comprehensive community care center or fifteen visits to a private practitioner), home health services (one hundred visits per year), post-hospital extended care (one hundred days per year), well-child care (to age six) and eye, ear, and dental care for children (up to age thirteen).

Population Coverage. The CHIP plan, while calling for voluntary enrollment, would provide for complete coverage at no premium cost for all individuals with incomes below $3,500 or families with incomes below $5,000. Thus, the program would drastically improve coverage for the many poor individuals and families not currently covered under Medicaid. An additional $4 billion would be spent on services rendered to the poor alone. The plan would eliminate current discrimination against single individuals, childless couples, and male-headed families and those inequities inherent in state control over eligibility criteria. However, for individuals or families above the income levels noted above, premiums would increase from zero to $120 or $300, respectively. Many individuals or families may find themselves unable to afford these premiums and will choose to remain uncovered. They would then forego the use of needed health services, bear the full costs of health care, or receive care on a charitable basis when available.

Cost Sharing. The AHIP component of the CHIP plan would incorporate premiums, deductibles, coinsurance rates, and limits to liability which increase with income. No premium would be imposed on families with less than $5,000 income or on individuals with an income of less than $3,500. Premiums would increase to maximums of $360 for individuals with income of $7,000 or more and to $900 for families with $10,000 income or more. The highest premiums would in most cases be paid by high risk individuals. Individuals with incomes of these levels who are employed would be better off by choosing coverage under EHIP. Individuals who are not employed and not high risks could purchase individual policies at lower rates than under AHIP. Deductibles would begin at zero and rise to $50 for prescription drugs and $150 for all other services for individuals with incomes over $7,000 and families with incomes over $10,000. Deductibles would be imposed on each family member up to a maximum of three. Liabilty for expenditures would be limited to 6 percent of income for individuals with incomes less than $1,750 and families with income less than $2,500. Maximum liability rates would increase to 15 percent of income for individuals with income over $5,250 and families with income over $7,500. Maximum liability would be no greater than $1,050 for an individual and $1,500 for a family. Premiums, deductibles, coinsurance rates and limits on liability are shown in Table 5-1.

Table 5-1
Premiums and Cost Sharing in the Administration's Assisted Health Insurance Plan

Annual Income of Single Individual	Premium	Deductibles (Per Person) Drugs	Others	Coinsurance Rates	Maximum Liability
$ 0 - $1,749	0	0	0	10%	6% of Income
1,750 - 3,499	0	25	50	15	9% of Income
3,500 - 5,249	120	50	100	20	12% of Income
5,250 - 6,999	240	50	150	25	15% of Income
7,000 - +	360	50	150	25	$1,050
Annual Income of Family	Premium	Drugs	Others	Coinsurance Rates	Maximum Liability
$ 0 - $2,499	0	0	0	10%	6% of Income
2,500 - 4,999	0	25	50	15	9% of Income
5,000 - 7,499	300	50	100	20	12% of Income
7,500 - 9,999	600	50	150	25	15% of Income
10,000 - +900		50	150	25	$1,500

While the Assisted Health Insurance plan follows principles which are designed to promote efficiency and equity, premiums, deductibles, and coinsurance escalate with income at rates which appear excessively steep. This is undesirable for two reasons. First, significant "notch" effects are created as individuals whose incomes increase face high "taxes" in the form of premiums (when the $5,000 level is crossed), and larger deductibles and coinsurance payments. Marginal tax rates are increased to the point that might adversely affect work effort. Second, the cost sharing provisions may do little to relieve the harsh burden of medical expenses of many low-income people. Families and individuals presently covered by Medicaid currently pay nothing for services covered by the program in their state. Such persons would make significant cutbacks in their use of services or would face major increases in their medical care outlays. Others not presently covered by any program will certainly be better off but will still be faced with outlays which seem large in relation to income.

To illustrate the effects of the Assisted Health Insurance plan, we examined three hypothetical four-person families assuming the families have "low" ($400), "medium" ($900) and "high" ($2,000) costs.[b] In this plan, the outlays of a family depend not only on total costs but the distribution of medical expenses among family members. Under the provisions of the plan, the greater the share

[b]In the following pages, costs will refer to total medical care costs incurred by the family. Outlays will refer to that portion of total medical care costs paid by the family.

of family medical costs incurred on behalf of one person, the less the share of total medical care costs faced by the family because deductibles will be lower and coinsurance payments higher. This assumes two other family members meet the deductible. Three persons must meet the deductible before coverage begins for other family members. If medical care costs are fairly equally distributed with no members reaching the deductible, the family will bear all costs up to its maximum liability. That is, if all members of a five-person, $6,000 income family have medical care costs of $95, total family outlays will be $475. In our hypothetical families, costs are assumed to be primarily incurred by one member. We have not found family outlays to be drastically affected if they are assumed to be more evenly distributed. Hypothetical costs are given in Table 5-2 for each member in each of three families.

Outlays that each of the hypothetical families would incur at four different income levels are shown in Table 5-3. Outlays borne by families with income of $1500 would be very low in relation to income. However, there are relatively few such families. In 1972, there were 1.2 million families (4.1 million persons) with less than $1,500 income and 2.8 million families (9.8 million persons) with less than $2,500 income [48]. Families with income between $2,500 and $5,000 would begin to have fairly large outlays for medical care. Families with $3,000 income would have outlays of almost 7.5 percent of income even with low ($400) total medical care costs. Families with income of $3,000 with average ($900) costs would pay $270—the maximum liability imposed on any family with that income. Thus, a large percentage of families who currently pay nothing under Medicaid would, under the new plan, pay 9 percent of income for medical care.[c]

While most national health insurance plans will be some combination of pure insurance and subsidization of the poor and ill, it is notable that in the CHIP

Table 5-2
Medical Care Outlays for Three Hypothetical Families

Family Member	Low Medical Care Cost Family ($400)		Average Medical Care Cost Family ($900)		High Medical Care Cost Family ($2,000)	
	Drugs	Other	Drugs	Other	Drugs	Other
1	$25	$210	$60	$600	$130	$1,630
2	5	50	10	70	10	70
3	5	50	10	70	10	70
4	5	50	10	70	10	70

[c]An interesting but unavoidable feature of the plan is that, within an income bracket, outlays borne by the family would increase in absolute amounts but decline as a percentage of income as medical care costs increased. Thus, a family with average expenses would pay $270, or 9 percent, with a $3,000 income, but $308, or 6.8 percent, if its income were $4,500.

Table 5-3

Medical Care Outlays (Including Premiums) Paid by Four-Person Family Under CHIP Plan

Family Income	Low Medical Care Cost Family ($400)	Average Medical Care Cost Family ($900)	High Medical Care Cost Family ($2,000)
$1,500 - A[2]	$ 40 (2.7%)	$ 90 (6.0%)	$ 90 (6.0%)
3,000 - A[2]	222 (7.4%)	270 (9.0%)	270 (9.0%)
4,500 - A[2]	222 (4.9%)	309 (6.8%)	405 (9.0%)
6,000 - E[1,3]	505 (8.4%)	697 (11.6%)	900 (15.0%)
6,000 - A[2]	612 (10.2%)	792 (13.2%)	1,012 (16.9%)
7,500 - E[1,3]	505 (6.7%)	697 (9.2%)	980 (13.1%)
7,500 - A[2]	955 (12.7%)	1,147 (15.3%)	1,430 (19.1%)

1. E—Employee Health Care Insurance Plan
2. A—Assisted Health Care Insurance Plan
3. If the employer's share of the premium required under the Employee Health Care Insurance Plan is shifted backward onto labor, the actual outlay of the family will be increased by $450, which is 75% of the expected average premium of $600.

plan the subsidy component quickly recedes at income levels above $5,000. At income levels of $5,000, a big increase in family outlays occurs in the AHIP plan, principally because of the $300 premium. For most families, total outlays including premium will exceed total family medical care costs. In our example, low cost families with $6,000 income would, under the Assisted Health Care Insurance Plan, have outlays of $612, or 53 percent more than total medical care costs incurred. Average cost families with the same income would have outlays of $792, or 88 percent of total incurred medical care costs under the assisted plan.

Many families with $6,000 incomes would be covered under the Employee Health Care Insurance Plan. Because they would pay only 25 percent of their premium under EHIP, total family outlays including premiums would be a lower percentage of income, e.g., 11.6 percent of income for average cost families. However, if the employee's share of the premium required under this employee plan is shifted backward onto labor, the actual outlay of the family will be increased by $450, which is 75 percent of the expected average premium of $600. If the premium is shifted, most families around the $6,000 income level would have total outlays which exceed medical care costs.

An additional problem with the cost sharing features of the administration plan is the incentive it provides for the purchase of supplementary private insurance. As with Medicare, private insurance plans which would cover the deductibles and coinsurance liabilities would be offered. The actuarial value of these policies might be considerably less than their cost, but many families and individuals are likely to purchase them nonetheless. If middle and upper income families purchase private insurance to cover the deductible and coinsurance liabilities, much of the incentive built into the plan to discourage excessive utilization will be lost. In addition, higher income families could end up facing lower marginal costs at time of use than low income families who cannot afford to purchase supplementary insurance. If supplementary insurance is purchased by significant numbers of people, neither the goals of equity nor efficiency would be achieved. One way to reduce the purchase of supplementary policies is to eliminate the federal subsidies to corporations for contributions to supplementary insurance as well as the deductions for health insurance in the individual income tax.

Reimbursement. Another serious problem with the CHIP plan is that the method of reimbursing physicians in the plan could create different incentives for providing care to the poor vis-à-vis the non-poor. The program would classify physicians as full-participating providers, associate-participating providers, and non-participating providers. Full-participating providers would agree to accept reimbursement from the government as full payment for services rendered. In exchange, the program would bill eligible families for their cost sharing liabilities. Associate-participating providers would accept reimbursement from the government as full payment for AHCIP and Medicare patients and for the insured portion in the employee program, but would bill the patient directly for the uninsured portion of the latter plus any supplemental charge. Non-participating providers could not be reimbursed for any service. The problem with this classification arrangement is that it gives clear incentive for physicians to provide preferential treatment to employed patients willing to pay a supplement to the required cost sharing. Incentives are created that would lead some physicians to refuse to see poor and aged patients and for others to render a lower level of service quality. In addition, individual states will control reimbursement policy, with the result that some states will provide generous reimbursement and others will be quite stringent. The inevitable outcome, judging from the Medicaid experience, is that the incentives providers have to treat the poor will vary widely across states.

It should be noted that the poor will benefit in the CHIP plan in that providers in either the full or associated classification cannot charge AHIP or FHIP beneficiaries more than the rates set by the states. Greater movement toward elimination of incentives to treat rich and poor differently would probably require physicians to either accept rates set by the government or forfeit any reimbursement at all for those services, as in Great Britain. Such a step would undoubtedly render the program unacceptable to the medical community and to many others as well.

Administration. In the effort to gain the equity and efficiency benefits inherent in variable cost sharing arrangements, the plan may face severe administrative problems in making determinations of family income. Such determinations are necessary to assign appropriate premiums, deductibles, and coinsurance rates. For many individuals, especially the poor and near poor, incomes vary widely from year to year and within a year. A family may have a $6,000 income in one year and a lower level, say $3,000, the next. Its premiums, deductibles, and coinsurance rates would be established on the basis of the higher level of income in the first year, but the family's ability to pay would have fallen in the second year in which those rates were applicable. Other families may experience substantial income variations within a calendar year. Adjustments of premiums, deductibles, coinsurance, and maximum liability would need to be made with each income change. Such adjustments would be taxing for the administrative machinery and would create confusion and frustration for those families whose incomes are subject to frequent change.

A second administrative problem stems from the voluntary nature of the plan. When insurance is voluntary, many individuals and families may choose not to participate. For example, families with over $5,000 in income may not be willing to pay $300 for coverage. Such freedom of choice has certain desirable characteristics in terms of maintaining personal liberty but may involve serious problems of bill collection when persons who choose not to participate incur large medical bills. It would introduce the necessity of sanctions on those who incur large expenses which they are unable to pay. It would be difficult politically to systematically impose harsh penalties on such people. Yet weak penalties such as loans at market interest rates may create incentives for many individuals to choose against participation. This would be especially likely to occur for those groups for whom expected benefits (expected costs of medical care utilization less cost sharing) are less than expected costs (premiums plus taxes and cost sharing).

Financing. Poor families below $5,000 will not finance a disproportionate share of program costs. However, as noted above, the $300 premium for families between $5,000 and $7,500 is a significant "notch" which may adversely affect work effort. Families could avoid the $300 premium by choosing coverage under EHCIP but would face larger deductibles and coinsurance rates and have a greater maximum liability. In addition, firms in low wage industries may find premiums (which, unlike payroll taxes, are not related to wages) a severe burden. Employers should be able to shift premiums for high wage individuals backward onto employees [8]. However, the ability of the firm to shift the premium backward is clearly limited by the minimum wage. As a result, there may be a reduction in demand for less skilled workers and greater incentives to employ temporary and part-time workers for whom employers do not make premium payments. Subsidies are designed to alleviate the burden on such employers, but if they are set at insufficient levels, premiums could seriously reduce opportunities for employment for low income individuals.

The Health Security Act (Kennedy-Griffiths)

The Kennedy-Griffiths bill would establish a national health insurance program with universal coverage and a broad range of services. Services covered include hospital inpatient care, psychiatric hospital inpatient care (sixty-five days in spell of illness), skilled nursing home care (one hundred and twenty days in spell of illness), outpatient care, physicians services, psychiatrists services (limited to twenty visits if private physician), dental services (up to age fifteen in beginning and gradually extended to rest of population), podiatry, home health services, lab and X-ray, medical appliances, and ambulance services. Prescription drugs are provided for chronic conditions, but without limitation if provided by HMO or foundation. Cost-sharing would not be imposed on any service, thus eliminating any financial barrier to access to care.

Cost sharing, reimbursement and administration. Cost increases would be constrained by federal control over the annual budget for health services. Each year a national health budget for the coming year would be determined on the basis of current costs, adjusted for changes in prices, population and the capacity of the delivery system. Funds would be allocated to each region on the basis of expected per capita utilization for each institution, physician services, dental services, drugs, etc. Hospitals and skilled nursing homes would be expected to provide all needed care for the allocated amount. HMOs and professional foundations would also receive a per capita amount for enrolled persons for ambulatory care based on the per capita allocation in their region. If they provide hospital and/or skilled nursing home care, they would receive payments for expected utilization of these services as well. Physicians and other private practitioners could choose to be paid on a fee-for-service basis, capitation or salary. However, allocations from the pre-determined fund could be first made to providers accepting capitation or salary. Payments to physicians choosing fee-for-service would be limited by the pre-determined budget and if payments exceed estimated levels, fees would be reduced. The latter is intended to provide strong incentives for physicians to accept capitation or to enter HMOs or foundations.

One clear objective of the bill is to eliminate differences in utilization attributable to differences in ability to pay. The plan also envisions a redistribution of medical resources to currently underserved areas, thus attempting to eliminate differences in utilization attributable to variations in availability of care. While the plan seems particularly well-designed to meet the needs of low income families and individuals, there are reasons to be concerned with its effects on the poor. First, it is the intention of the plan that decisions affecting the rationing of scarce supplies be made by providers and not by the price mechanism. However, with no premium contributions and no cost sharing by any family or individual regardless of income, the program will have a high budget cost if all services desired by patients at zero price are to be provided. While providers will have strong incentives to control utilization because of prepayment, the threat that consumers can choose other providers with no cost to themselves may limit their willingness to exercise that control. That is, there is no incentive for consumers to seek the most efficient provider. This may result in pressure on providers to deliver more care than that which is permitted by the pre-determined budget. If Congress permits budgets to be set at levels which permit providers to deliver all or most of the care desired at zero price, large increases in income and payroll tax contributions would be required. Consumption of other goods and services would be given up to finance use of medical services that would not be demanded if cost sharing were employed. If large health expenditures are not wholly financed through tax increases, funds will necessarily be allocated to health services from other government programs. Programs which are eliminated may very likely finance income transfers or services, i.e., housing, education, which are more valuable than those health services for which there is a demand only when provided free.

Alternatively, if Congress chooses to limit funds below the level required to induce provision of desired services, severe problems of access for the poor may develop. The intense debate over the size of the federal budget in past years suggests that the level of the health budget would continually be subject to political pressure. If the size of the federal health budget significantly constrains capitation payments, limitations in services, queues, and reduction in quality will necessarily occur. While priorities may be assigned by providers to those most in need, such an outcome is not assured. If capitation payments do not accurately reflect the expected value of medical care costs of each patient, providers will have an incentive to discourage relatively high risks. Private physicians are apparently not required to accept anyone as a patient; as a result, they have an incentive to avoid high risks as long as there is reason to believe costs of care will exceed the capitation payment or total fee reimbursements. HMOs and foundations are required to accept anyone who wishes to enroll. However, they have an incentive to provide relatively high risks with low quality of service to reduce the cost of care below the capitation payment. If the patient seeks an alternative provider, the HMO or foundation merely loses a patient whose cost of care exceeded the capitation payment. On the other hand, HMOs and foundations have an incentive to provide relatively low risks with a high quality of service as long as the capitation payment exceeds the cost of care of that quality. Since HMOs and foundations must provide open enrollment, high risk individuals will find an organization willing to provide some level of care. Unfortunately, it is likely to be within an HMO specializing in low quality care to high risks or a low quality of care within an HMO with a broad mix of risks. The current Medicaid population contains a significant percentage of these high risks: the indigent aged and disabled, mothers in childbearing years, and young children in low income families.

The poor are likely to receive a lower quality of care even if capitation payments accurately reflect the expected value of medical care costs. Providers would have an incentive to maximize the quantity and quality of service within their budget constraint because of the threat of loss of patients for whom they are paid a capitation amount. They might, therefore, limit the care provided to each patient to that permitted by the capitation payment. Since care needs are unpredictable over a short period of time, say a year, such a policy in practice would be merely one of non-discrimination among patients. But providers faced with limited budgets may find it worthwhile to restrict the quantity and quality of service to those least likely to seek alternatives. These will, in most cases, be those who are less mobile and have less access to information, i.e., the aged, disabled, and poor.

Finally, the administrative tasks faced by the program would be awesome. If it proves difficult to operate the program administratively, as seems inevitable, it may become impossible to control supplemental payments by middle and high income groups in return for preferential treatment. The poor, who are less able to pay a monetary price for preferred status, will pay by waiting or by receiving lower quality health care.

Financing. The Kennedy-Griffiths bill is financed through a combination of payroll taxes and general revenues. Payroll taxes are proportional up to certain established income levels and regressive beyond. It is unfortunate that still another federal program would be financed through this mechanism rather than, say, the personal income tax. However, the combination of payroll taxes and general revenues proposed in the Kennedy-Griffiths bill is quite progressive relative to financing mechanisms in other plans.

*The Comprehensive National Health
Insurance Act (Kennedy-Mills)*

The Kennedy-Mills bill calls for a national health insurance program with comprehensive health care benefits provided to all families and individuals who contribute. All persons presently covered under the present Social Security program and their dependents would be eligible for benefits. New entrants to the work force, not fully or currently insured, would also be covered during the first week of work of twenty-five hours or more. Families receiving AFDC benefits would also be eligible. Services covered under the plan include inpatient hospital services, physician services, home health services (one hundred visits per year), post-hospital extended care services (one hundred days per year), inpatient mental health services (thirty full or sixty partial days), outpatient mental health services,[d] outpatient prescription drugs and preventive care services, including:

---

[d]This benefit is limited to cost of thirty visits—to a private practitioner or outpatient services of a private practitioner equal to half the cost of thirty visits.

routine dental, eye and ear care for children under age thirteen; well-child care to age six; prenatal care; and family planning services. The plan also contains extensive provisions for a long-term care program for the elderly, a program which is carefully avoided by other national health insurance plans.

Population Coverage. A major problem with the Kennedy-Mills plan is that many poor families and individuals would be excluded from coverage. While the plan is generous in its treatment of most low income individuals, those who are unemployed or not in the labor force who are not eligible for an income transfer program would not be covered. Migrant workers; part-time, casual, and multiple employer workers; domestics; and others not a dependent of someone fully or currently insured under Social Security would often not be covered. This would include many of the single individuals, childless couples, and male-headed families presently excluded from Medicaid.

Cost Sharing. The cost sharing features of the plan are similar in some ways to the CHIP plan but are considerably more generous in their treatment of low income families and individuals. No deductibles or cost sharing would be imposed on any individual or family at or below the following levels of income:

Family Size	Income
Individual	$2,400
Two-Person Family	3,600
Three-Person Family	4,200
Four-Person Family	4,800
Five or More Person Families	4,800 + 400 for each additional member

All services other than preventive care services would be subject to a per person deductible of $150. No family would be required to meet more than two deductibles. After meeting the deductibles, the family would pay 25 percent of all medical care costs. Prescription drugs (outpatient) are excluded from the provisions stated above, but would be subject to a payment of $1 per prescription. Maximum liability is determined by family size and income. No family (of four) with income over $8,800 would be responsible for more than $1,000 of medical care costs. Four-person families with income between $4,800 and $8,800 would have maximum liabilities equal to 25 percent of the difference between their income and $4,800. Thus, a family with $7,200 income would never have medical care outlays exceeding $600.

Cost sharing under the Kennedy-Mills proposal would place very limited burdens on the poor. The same hypothetical families used in our description of the CHIP plan were used in the development of Table 5-4. That is, the same

Table 5-4

Medical Care Outlays (Including Contributions) Paid by Four-Person Family Under Kennedy-Mills Plan

| | Total Costs Incurred[1] | | |
Family Income	Low Medical Care Cost Family ($400)	Average Medical Care Cost Family ($900)	High Medical Care Cost Family ($2,000)
$1,500	$ 25 (1.7%)	$ 40 (2.7%)	$ 55 (3.7%)
3,000	40 (1.3%)	55 (1.8%)	70 (2.3%)
4,500	55 (1.2%)	70 (1.6%)	85 (1.9%)
6,000	360 (6.0%)	360 (6.0%)	360 (6.0%)
7,500	400 (5.3%)	573 (7.6%)	750 (10.0%)

1. If payroll taxes are shifted backward onto labor, total family outlays would increase by 3% of income for each family. Likewise, if the 3% tax on state AFDC benefits is shifted onto recipients, outlays of families receiving unearned income would also be higher than 3% of income.

distribution of expenses over the members of a four-person family detailed in Table 5-1 is assumed. As is readily discernible from Table 5-4, families under $4,800 of income would be liable for only the costs of outpatient drugs. Cost sharing rises rapidly above $4,800 because families become liable for two $150 per person deductibles and the 25 percent coinsurance. While cost sharing liabilities increase rapidly as income increases, they are well below those imposed on families with similar incomes under the CHIP plan. Nonetheless, the rates at which family outlays rise with income may create severe notch effects. For example, families with average medical expenses ($900) would have an increase in outlays of $290 if income increased from $4,500 to $6,000. In addition, if all family income were earned, payroll taxes would increase by $60 (assuming payroll taxes are shifted onto workers). Thus, the increase in the combined marginal tax rate would be 23.3 percent. This notch problem could be alleviated only if low coinsurance rates were imposed on those below $4,800 and both deductibles and coinsurance rates increased at slower rates as income increases.

A final issue with the cost sharing features of the Kennedy-Mills plan concerns the lack of incentives for low income families to be conscious of the cost of services. It is not necessarily desirable that care be provided with no cost sharing for all families and individuals below the income levels specified by the plan. Such provisions can result in over-utilization and higher costs. As mentioned earlier, routine "first dollar" medical care is no more urgent than food or housing, which are not 100 percent subsidized. The designers of plan for financing health care services for the poor should be concerned with the value to their clients of programs which will be foregone because of expenditures on health services. In particular, one should be concerned with whether those services not provided are more valuable to the poor than those health services which would not be used because of imposition of low cost sharing provisions such as coinsurance rates of 10 to 15 percent. In the case of the Kennedy-Mills plan, the designers clearly envision a tax on unearned income of AFDC recipients and on state AFDC budgets. Thus, health services which will be used because there is no coinsurance requirement are in effect substituted for cash assistance to the same families.

Reimbursement. The Kennedy-Mills plan contains a physician reimbursement provision somewhat similar to that in the CHIP plan. By choosing to participate in the program, physicians agree to accept payments from the government which are set by fee schedules in exchange for government collection of deductibles and coinsurance from the patient. Or, by choosing not to participate, physicians can collect the government share of the allowed fee from the government and bill the patient for his cost sharing liability plus any supplemental charges the physicians can collect. Unlike the CHIP proposal, physicians could charge the poor more than rates determined by the government by choosing not to participate. As with CHIP, such arrangements can lead to two classes of patients because physicians have obvious incentives to provide preferential treatment to those patients able to pay supplements to the required cost sharing. Some physicians will treat the middle and upper classes and others will care for the poor. The theory presumably is that such schemes are unavoidable if the program is to guarantee physician support and avoid illicit covert payments by those willing and able to pay for preferred status.

Administration. The Kennedy-Mills plan would also face the problems confronting the CHIP proposal of supplementation by purchasing private insurance policies to cover deductibles and coinsurance liabilities and the administrative problems of income determination. Neither is likely to be as much a problem under Kennedy-Mills as under the CHIP plan. Because the maximum liability is lower under Kennedy-Mills than under CHIP, fewer families will find it beneficial to purchase supplementary plans. Thus, the effects of the cost sharing provisions on utilization are less likely to be diluted.

Problems of income determination will be as difficult under Kennedy-Mills as under CHIP, but the consequences of errors will be less pronounced. The plan has no premium, and deductibles and coinsurance rates are only affected by one income change, when income increases to exceed $4,800 (for a four person family). The necessity of periodic adjustments of premiums, deductibles, etc., will not be as severe as with CHIP.

Financing. The Kennedy-Mills plan is basically financed through the payroll tax mechanism. Payroll taxes will be imposed on 4 percent of annual earnings up to $20,000 per year. Employers would be responsible for at least 3 percent and employees for no more than 1 percent. However, economic theory and empirical research suggest that the entire tax will be shifted onto employees [8]. Thus the Kennedy plan would be financed with a tax mechanism that will be proportional up to $20,000 and regressive thereafter. The working families with $6,000 incomes in Table 5-4 will pay an additional $240 per year in payroll taxes. The payroll tax also imposes penalties on families with more than one worker. In addition, AFDC benefits would be taxed at the rate of 1 percent on the recipient and 3 percent on the state. The latter 3 percent may eventually be passed on to the welfare recipient via lower levels of cash assistance.

Catastrophic Health Insurance and Medical Assistance Reform Act (Long-Ribicoff)

The Long-Ribicoff proposal would combine a plan for catastrophic insurance for the general population and greater regulation of the private insurance industry with a plan for low income families. The plan for the poor would essentially be a completely federal Medicaid program with universal coverage of all persons below certain income levels with a wide range of benefits. Program benefits would be available to all whose annual family income is below the amounts specified below:

Individual	$2,400
Two-Person Family	3,600
Three-Person Family	4,200
Four-Person Family	4,800
Five or More Person Families	4,800 + $400 for each additional member

Benefits included in the program include inpatient hospital services (sixty-day limit), skilled nursing care, intermediate care, physician services, laboratory and X-ray, home health services, prenatal and well-baby care, periodic examinations (for children under eighteen), outpatient physical therapy, immunizations and pap smears, medical supplies, and ambulance services.

Cost sharing. Cost sharing would be limited to $3 per visit for the first ten outpatient visits. Thus the financial burden on any poor family or individual would be very low. Unfortunately such limited cost sharing provisions result in serious "notch" effects when family income exceeds the level stated above. The plan provides for a "spend-down" provision similar to that in the Medicaid program (see Chapter 2). Under this provision, a family is eligible for coverage once its annual income minus its total medical expenses is less than the income levels stated above. For example, a family of four with an annual income of $5,500 would be covered once its total medical expenses exceed $700. Such a provision is valuable only in that there is some limit to the catastrophe which a family can suffer. In actuality, the spend-down operates as a very severe income related deductible. The Long-Ribicoff plan appears to assume that families above $4,800 will purchase private insurance policies which would have no more than a $100 hospital deductible and $200 of medical care cost sharing. Current experience with private insurance suggests that many families with incomes in the $5,000 to $10,000 range will not buy such policies. Premiums would presumably cost over $300 per family for policies with the cost sharing provisions mentioned above. Thus, even though family liability will be limited by the spend down provision, family health care expenses will escalate rapidly as income increases above the designated income eligibility levels.

Reimbursement. The Long-Ribicoff bill proposes to reimburse physicians for reasonable charges and hospitals on a reasonable cost basis. The problems with these forms of reimbursement are well known and are described in Chapter 2. With minimal cost sharing and reimbursement arrangements which are limited in their ability to constrain costs, the Long-Ribicoff bill could become extremely expensive. That part of the plan which finances care for the poor will certainly exceed the costs of comparable components of the three alternatives discussed above. The major difficulty with large expenditures on health services for the poor is that other services which are valuable to the poor may be foregone. If expenditures for pollution control, housing, food, etc., are reduced to finance an expensive health services program for the poor, the welfare and perhaps even the health of the same individuals may be reduced.

Despite the employment of relatively generous reimbursement schemes for providers of services to the poor, the Long-Ribicoff plan proposes that charges for services to the non-poor could be even higher. Thus, like the CHIP and Kennedy-Mills proposal, the plan would create different incentives for providing preferential treatment to the non-poor.

Administration. The spend-down provision is difficult to administer because of problems of income determination. It is also extremely confusing to families whose incomes are above the designated cutoff levels. Under the present Medicaid program, there are an unknown number of families who fail to understand the provisions of the program and/or fail to make precise determinations of their own income. As a result, they do not make use of their eligibility for Medicaid coverage. The same problem would most likely plague the implementation of the Long-Ribicoff plan.

Financing. The Long-Ribicoff plan for low income families and individuals would be financed through contributions from the states equal to the state's present payments under the Medicaid program for those services covered by the

Long-Ribicoff plan. In addition, for services covered by the Long-Ribicoff plan, the state would be required to pay one-half the payments it would have made if its eligibility requirements had been the same under the new plan. There seems to be no particular justification for this financing mechanism other than the fact that it is based on the Medicaid arrangements presently in use and its continuance would avoid giving revenues back to the states. Under this arrangement the effect on the poor will vary by state, depending on the size of the state contribution and its methods of generating revenues. States which generate a large proportion of their revenues from sales taxes will place relatively large burdens on the poor for financing the health care program. This will be particularly true in states with a large number of individuals eligible for the Long-Ribicoff plan and a low federal matching rate under the present Medicaid program. The poor in states with relatively small numbers of eligibles and/or high federal matching rates under Medicaid, coupled with progressive state taxation schemes, would bear relatively mild burdens under the new plan.

Coverage of Long-Term Care in National Health Insurance

Most national health insurance plans exclude coverage of long-term care. Long-term care is normally defined to refer to nursing homes, related facilities, and home care provided to functionally impaired individuals. The definition often includes homes for the retarded, mental hospitals, and chronic disease hospitals. Medicaid will currently finance long-term treatment in skilled nursing and intermediate care facilities. It contains provisions for home health care, but this service is denied to persons with stabilized chronic rather than acute conditions. Any reform of the Medicaid program would have to incorporate provisions for long-term care.

Problems in the present structure of long-term care financing fall into four overlapping categories: (1) care is often unavailable for those in need; (2) individuals receive care in institutions when non-institutional care would be more appropriate; (3) long-term care imposes enormous financial burdens on individuals and their families with insurance protection being either too costly or unavailable; and (4) care provided under existing arrangements is often of mediocre quality.

The Administration plan would continue to provide under Medicaid certain long-term care services including: care in a skilled nursing facility or intermediate care facility, care in mental institution for persons under twenty-one or over sixty-five; and home health services. The Kennedy-Griffiths plan would only provide skilled nursing care, psychiatric hospital inpatient care, and home health services when related to a specific illness. The Kennedy-Mills bill would establish a long-term program which would cover non-institutional medical and social services and long-term institutional care when medically necessary. The Long-Ribicoff bill would extend the long-term care services currently provided under Medicaid to the expanded number of individuals eligible for that plan.

While we will not analyze long-term care financing in any detail, some issues are worthy of mention. First, more adequate provision for long-term care of the elderly may be quite expensive. Total expenditures for nursing home care in 1970 were $2.8 billion, of which 64 percent was financed by government [57]. Providing care for those who require but do not now receive institutional care, and improvements in the quality of care would both increase the level of these outlays. More adequate provision of home care might reduce the costs of caring for some persons now inappropriately institutionalized. But home care would generally add to long-term care costs through the provision of care to persons who now receive no care or inadequate care in the community. Second, much of a long-term care package (e.g., care in a nursing home) substitutes for, rather than adds to, the services which individuals normally require. Thus because a nursing home provides housing, nutrition, and other services, a resident faces significantly reduced normal living expenses when in a nursing home. As a consequence, the user charges imposed on long-term care (particularly institutional charges) can reasonably absorb signficantly larger shares of patient income than is the case with acute care. Thus ceilings on total patient expenses which are appropriate for acute care may be inappropriate when applied to long-term institutional care.

Third, acute medical care has relatively few close substitutes. Long-term care services, on the other hand, substitute for regularly consumed goods and services and for care provided informally by spouses and other relatives and friends. Demands for such services may therefore be quite expansive and may justify higher user charges than are imposed on acute care services. It should also be noted that these points relate differentially to patients with and without spouses and consequently charges may usefully be varied with family status as well as income and other variables.[3]

Summary

Several issues—of particular importance to the poor—in national health insurance plans require greater consideration than they have received to date. We began by observing that cost sharing provisions should be limited so that the burden on the poor and near-poor are not high in relation to income. We also argued that cost sharing should not be so low that (1) excessive utilization is encouraged and (2) sharp "notch" effects occur when cost sharing is imposed on higher income groups. We showed that the Administration's CHIP plan contains cost sharing features which were quite high in relation to income. For example, families with $3,000 incomes with average total medical care costs would have medical care outlays equal to 9 percent of income. The Long-Ribicoff plan, while generous in its treatment of families below income levels of $4,800 (for four-person families), includes a spend-down feature which could result in large outlays for families with incomes which are not significantly greater than $4,800. The absence of cost sharing for low income groups in the Kennedy-Griffiths, Kennedy-Mills, and Long-Ribicoff plans could mean that programs which would be quite valuable to the poor would not receive federal support. There has not been adequate consideration in the design of these plans of the issue of whether those programs not provided are more valuable to the poor than those health services which would not be used because of the imposition of a reasonable cost sharing arrangement. We also observed that sharp "notch" effects occur in the Kennedy-Mills and Long-Ribicoff proposals, principally because they attempt to integrate the absence of cost sharing for the poor with rather significant cost sharing for the near-poor and the rest of the population.

Reimbursement arrangements under the CHIP, Kennedy-Mills, and Long-Ribicoff plans provide for implicit incentives for providers to treat the poor and non-poor differently. Reimbursement policy under the Long-Ribicoff plan seems inadequately concerned with cost control. Provider reimbursement under the Kennedy-Griffiths plan, while concerned with cost control, would be difficult to administer efficiently and may lead to creation of incentives which would adversely affect the poor.

Programs which employ income related cost sharing (e.g., CHIP) may have to face difficult problems of income determination. Plans using a spend-down as an income-related catastrophic insurance plan (e.g., Long-Ribicoff) will also have difficult income determination problems. Plans with income-related cost sharing or spend-down features will have to provide sufficient information so that the program is comprehensible to the less sophisticated members of society. Plans with voluntary coverage (e.g., CHIP) will have to develop procedures for imposing sanctions on individuals who choose not to participate but incur large medical bills they are unable to pay.

The Kennedy-Mills and Kennedy-Griffiths proposals lean heavily on payroll taxes to finance covered services. They call for increasing the tax base for the payroll tax to lessen its regressivity. Yet, it is unfortunate, given recent evidence of the fairly proportional incidence of the entire tax system [34], that greater consideration is not given to use of more progressive taxes such as the individual income tax. Despite this objection, use of payroll taxes has several advantages over the premium contributions called for in the CHIP plan. Premiums under the employee plan (EHCIP) will be based on risks and will not be related to income. Thus, contributions will be a much greater share of income for low income families than for high income families. The CHIP plan also has the disadvantage that firms will have incentives to hire part-time rather than full-time workers in order to avoid health insurance contributions and to hire "low risk" individuals rather than "high risk" individuals to minimize health insurance costs.

Notes

1. For evidence that deductibles and coinsurance affect utilization of medical services, see C.F. Phelps and J.P. Newhouse, "The Effects of Coinsurance on Demand for Physician Services," Office of Economic Opportunity, 1972.

2. For a more thorough analysis of issues raised by various plans, see Karen Davis, "National Health Insurance," in Barry M. Bleckman et al., *Setting National Priorities: the 1975 Budget* (Washington, D.C.: The Brookings Institution, 1974).

3. For a more lengthy discussion of issues in long-term care organization and finance, see William Pollak et al., "Federal Long-Term Care Strategy: Options and Analysis," Urban Institute Working Paper 970-04-01, October 1973.

6 Increasing the Efficiency of the System

Any of the plans described in Chapter 5 would provide a rather large subsidy to those who currently are without coverage. One plan, the CHIP proposal, would decrease the value of the subsidy to those whose care is currently fully subsidized. The net effect of any of the plans would probably be a significant increase in demand for hospital, medical, and other services. Indeed, that is the purpose of national health insurance. Unfortunately, increasing access of the poor and others to health services cannot be done without adding to inflationary pressures which exist even at present levels of coverage. Reform of the present program for financing of care for the poor will greatly intensify the need for measures to increase the efficiency of the delivery system.

There are several possible policies which might be adopted. First, there are various changes which could be made in the incentives and controls which face hospitals and physicians. For hospitals these would include prospective budgeting and incentive reimbursement. For physician practices, fee schedules could be employed in states currently reimbursing on the basis of customary and usual charges. Regional planning organizations could be strengthened to improve the allocation of capital resources, thus avoiding unnecessary capacity expansion and duplication of specialized resources. Utilization review can be used to control hospital admissions, length of stay, physician visits, and ancillary services. Second, there are alternative ways of organizing the financing and delivery of health services. Primarily, these include health maintenance organizations and medical society foundations. These organizational forms are alleged by many writers to increase the efficiency of medical practice. Because of prepayment on a capitation basis, these organizations face financial incentives to substitute ambulatory care for hospitalization, substitute less skilled for highly skilled personnel, and institute effective utilization review mechanisms.

Each of these policies may contribute significantly to increased efficiency and the lessening of inflationary pressures. Unfortunately, there seem to be critical problems associated with each. Because so little is currently known about the effectiveness of each of these alternative policy instruments, this chapter will be highly speculative. While no firm conclusions are drawn, two important points are emphasized. First, for potential gains in efficiency to be realized, it is essential that considerable care be taken in design and implementation of alternative policies. Second, the problems with each of these policies underscore the importance of equitable deductibles and coinsurance provisions in controlling costs.

Hospital Reimbursement

In Chapter 2 we argued that the present system of reimbursing hospitals on a reasonable cost basis provides little incentive for hospitals to operate efficiently. The result has been rising hospital prices which are absorbed by third parties and ultimately reflected in higher insurance premiums, taxes, and out-of-pocket payments. As a result, there has been considerable interest in recent years in alternative methods of reimbursement for hospital services.[1] Critics have suggested that hospitals be reimbursed on some prospective basis rather than through rates determined retrospectively, as is the current practice. There has been serious discussion of prospective or incentive reimbursement schemes, and experiments are in progress in several states.

Incentives can be structured in a variety of ways. One alternative is to reimburse hospitals on a capitation or per-enrollee basis. Under such an arrangement, hospitals would be paid a fixed annual amount per person to cover the needs of eligible persons in their jurisdictions. Since the level of receipts is fixed, hospitals have an incentive to operate in an economically efficient manner. A second method is to negotiate the budget of individual hospitals in advance, thereby inducing them to contain the total cost of operating the hospital for the coming year. Another procedure is to negotiate with the hospital a target rate based on present year's cost per day and a projected percentage increase or decrease in per diem costs. The negotiated rate would have to fall within a range established for the relevant hospital classification. Hospitals would then be given their actual daily cost plus some percentage of the difference between the target and their actual daily costs if they are below the target, and would receive their actual daily cost minus some percentage of the difference between the target and their unit costs if they are above the target. An alternative proposal would concentrate on cost increases by reimbursing hospitals by an amount corresponding to the average cost increases for all hospitals in the same classification in the community, regardless of their own cost increases [59]. Another would reimburse on the basis of outputs (defined as complete management of a medical condition) and would make payments a function of the difference between the cost (plus or minus a specified number of standard deviations) of treating a well-defined diagnosis in a relevant area and the actual cost [40]. While little objective information exists on the effectiveness of these proposals, each contains the potential for inducing economically efficient behavior. Inefficient hospitals would be penalized, while efficient hospitals would be rewarded. Hopefully, hospitals would develop, when economically warranted, extended care and home care services and the capacity to provide a wider range of services on an outpatient basis.

Despite the apparent advantages of incentive reimbursement schemes, very real problems exist. First, setting appropriate capitation rates is hampered by the difficulty of predicting utilization of groups of eligible individuals. Setting either capitation rates or budget targets for individual hospitals is also complicated by differences in size, specialized facilities, composition of medical staffs, and other characteristics. Second, capitation or predetermined annual budgets may induce reactions other than increased efficiency. Once the budget or capitation rate is determined, the income of the hospital is unrelated to the quantity or quality of care delivered. Dowling and others have argued that hospitals have incentives to reduce the number of admissions, length of stay or the level of amenities. They may also avoid difficult and expensive types of cases and reduce the intensity of service. It might be argued that quality would be maintained because of competition with other hospitals in the area, assuming eligibles could choose, say, once a year, among competing hospitals. However, if the patient's ability to make accurate judgments about service quality is limited, quality of hospital care may fall under either arrangement.

Several problems also exist with incentive systems based on target daily rates. First, establishing target rates is likely to be very difficult but, nonethless, critical to the success of the scheme. If the target is set too high, the increased payments to hospitals may be quite large and will provide rewards when little has been accomplished. Setting appropriate target rates is difficult because hospitals differ widely according to size, location, presence of teaching programs, case mix, composition of medical staff, etc. The treatment of capital expenditures is particularly complex. For example, should rates include compensation for existing specialized facilities which are unnecessary and are presently underutilized, particularly when other available facilities exist nearby?

A second problem is that incentive structures based on per diem rates may induce hospitals to specialize in less-complex and low-cost cases. Rafferty has found that substantial variation in case mix occurs among hospitals and within hospitals from month to month. He states that incentive reimbursement may

result in illusory gains if reduction in measured costs were achieved via real but unmeasured changes in the average product, in the form of subtle changes in the case-mix of admissions. . . . Such incentive could affect the pattern of future admissions in some degree by affecting hospital decisions regarding both the quantity and types of capital equipment they acquire, since the kinds of illnesses which can or cannot be effectively treated in the future will depend in part on these present decisions. [37]

A third problem is that average cost schemes, while introducing incentives for high-cost hospitals to be efficient, actually weaken the incentives for low-cost hospitals. For-profit hospitals may make intensive efforts to minimize costs and distribute the surplus generated by the incentive system to stockholders. However, non-profit hospitals, which probably maximize quality as well as income, are likely to use the additional income to invest in equipment, raise salaries, etc.—that is, make expenditure decisions which will eventually raise their costs [16, 32]. As costs of "low-cost" hospitals increase, the average cost base for the area will also increase. Incentive reimbursement schemes appear to be designed on the assumptions that hospitals are profit maximizers; but less than 15 percent of short-term hospital beds are in for-profit hospitals in the United States. Thus, incentive reimbursement may do little to curtail cost inflation, particularly if based on average costs.

Some problems are common to all prospective schemes. For example, as observed by Rafferty, since there are considerable differences in the degree to which individual hospitals can rely on philanthropy or community support, there will be considerable differences among hospitals in their responsiveness to any incentive scheme. Hospitals with ready access to philanthropic support may be relatively unresponsive to any incentive arrangement. Secondly, incentive reimbursement schemes are unlikely to affect hospital behavior if the sponsoring third party covers only part of the hospital's clientele. Incentive reimbursement will be far more effective under a single national program with universal coverage or under a coordinated effort by the major third parties—Medicare, Medicaid, and Blue Cross. Finally, most of the responsibility for use of hospital service lies with physicians, whose interests are not always aligned with the hospital. It is critical that hospitals gain control over physicians' behavior or that physicians also be faced with incentives which discourage unnecessary hospital use.

Physician Reimbursement

Finding methods of reimbursement for physicians and other providers which will encourage efficient behavior has been a critical and vexing problem for Medicaid and other public programs. Various alternative approaches to remuneration have been proposed by proponents of national health insurance schemes, and it appears this issue will be one of the more difficult to resolve. Under Medicaid several states reimburse physicians on the basis of "reasonable charges," which tend to give physicians considerable control over prices. It is frequently pointed out that this form of reimbursement (also followed by Medicare and private insurance carriers) contains no incentives for physicians to be efficient in the organization of their practice, in the choices of ancillary services, etc., and has generated considerable pressure on medical care prices. Because of the looseness of this arrangement, some states have instituted fairly tight maximum fees, allowing physicians flexibility within the maximum, while others have instituted rigorous fee schedules. Very little is known about the impact of these alternative reimbursement schemes on utilization and Medicaid costs. Do fee schedules reduce costs significantly or do physicians respond by prescribing greater amounts of discretionary services in order to attain a target income? Or do physicians respond by not participating as heavily in the program, seeing fewer patients and providing fewer services at perhaps lower quality? Are there differences in the utilization of services as well as in prices that can be attributed to different methods of reimbursement?

Speculation about the direction of physicians' responses to fee schedules which reduce the level of charges per unit of service is complicated by the fact that, unlike most goods or services, physicians have considerable control over the demand for their own services. There is also evidence of an excess demand for physicians' services. In either case, the volume of services provided can be increased in response to reduced fees if physicians choose to do so. Analysis is also complicated by the fact that the well-being of physicians appears to be positively affected by income, leisure, and the level of professional prestige (which is determined by the quality of care delivered) and negatively affected by the amount of entrepreneuring and management they need to perform. There is evidence that physicians are notoriously inefficient managers under current pricing arrangements. That is, they appear to prefer losses of income to acceptance of the burden of employment of their own time in organization of various available inputs (e.g., paraprofessional personnel) in an efficient manner to minimize production costs. Reinhardt [38] and others have provided evidence that the efficiency of physicians' practices could be increased by delivery of many services through greater use of personnel with lower levels of training and less use of physician time; others could argue that use of less-skilled personnel and less physician time would reduce service quality. For the purpose of this discussion, a reduction in inputs per unit of service (which would include substitution of lower- for higher-skilled personnel) would be a reduction in quality only if the result were a less-accurate diagnosis and/or a less appropriate treatment. If there were no change or an improvement in the accuracy of diagnosis and the appropriateness of treatment, there would be an increase in efficiency.

To recapitulate, physicians' responses will depend on trade-offs made among four variables: income, leisure, practice efficiency, and service quality. Because we know very little about physician behavior, it is difficult to make accurate predictions on the effects of fee schedules. Some of the potential physician responses include:

1. Accepting less income and increasing leisure (reduce own input), while maintaining current levels of efficiency and quality. This would reduce the volume of services but maintain quality.
2. Accepting less income and maintaining current level of own input, efficiency, and quality. This would hold both the quantity and quality of visits constant.
3. Accepting less income, but obtaining greater leisure by reducing quality, holding efficiency constant. Service quality would deteriorate, but the volume of contacts could increase or decrease or remain the same, depending on the relative impacts of reduced quality or increased leisure on the number of services provided.
4. Accepting less income, but obtaining greater leisure by increasing efficiency, holding quality constant. Quality would not deteriorate, but the volume of services could increase, decrease or remain the same, depending on the

relative effects of increasing efficiency and leisure on the number of services provided.

5. Maintaining same income by increasing own input (reducing leisure), while maintaining current levels of efficiency and quality. The number of services would increase, while service quality remains the same.

6. Maintaining same income, own work effort, and efficiency by reducing service quality. The number of services will increase, while quality deteriorates.

7. Maintaining same income, own work effort, and service quality by increasing efficiency. The number of services increases, while quality remains the same.

Clearly, options which maintain the quality and quantity of services are most socially desirable. Whether quality is maintained most likely depends on how averse the majority of physicians is to the provision of low-quality care. If this aversion tends to be strong, and physicians desire to maintain current standards of living (that is, current levels of income and leisure) increased efficiency could be the outcome of fee schedules. Physicians would then respond by increasing the number of services without a sacrifice of quality.

Unfortunately, there is little empirical evidence on the effects of fee schedules. Marmor [29] cites evidence of increased billing in Canada following imposition of fee schedules in national health insurance. In Chapters 3 and 4 of this study of Medicaid utilization, we examined the impacts of the three alternative schemes—reasonable charges, reasonable charges with maximum fees, and fee schedules—on the percentage of eligibles who use services and expenditures per use of the service. We found that the reimbursement arrangement has little effect on the percentage of eligibles using at least one service. This essentially reflects the patient's decision to seek care and, therefore, is not affected by reimbursement methods. On the other hand, the method of reimbursement had a strong impact on the level of expenditures per user of both hospital and medical services. Most of the effect on expenditures appeared to be due to lower charges. We observed little increase or decrease in quantity supplied and had no way of discerning changes in quality. We concluded that health care financing programs could obtain significant savings in costs under such programs as Medicare and Medicaid by employing fee schedules. However, such programs would incur the possible risk of adverse effects on the quality of services rendered their participants. The magnitude of this risk is unknown.

Area-wide Health Planning

The strengthening of comprehensive or area-wide planning organizations is often suggested as a means of inhibiting the growth of excess bed capacity and the unnecessary duplication of open heart surgery facilities, cobalt radiation units, etc. There has been great interest in and some empirical evidence for the proposition that an abundance of hospital beds leads to use of hospitals when lower cost alternatives are available [16].[a] The normal response to excess supply, in economic theory, is for a fall in price followed by an increase in demand. The fall in price would discourage any future expansion in bed supply, and perhaps encourage alternative uses for the existing excess capacity. However, in the hospital industry, it appears that suppliers do not reduce prices but attempt to directly influence demand to effect an increase in bed utilization. Providers are able to influence admission and discharge decisions principally because a large part of the U.S. population has broad insurance coverage of hospital costs and because patients are typically ignorant of the appropriate level of care. Klarman, for one, has suggested that the supply of beds be limited in order to ration utilization and control rising hospital costs [26]. Hospitals and physicians would have to allocate scarce beds among those patients most in need, postpone other cases until occupancy rates decrease and treat other cases on an outpatient basis.

The duplication of specialized facilities also contributes to excessive hospital costs. The fact that roughly 77 percent of all hospitals equipped to perform open-heart surgery performed less than one operation per week (in 1961) is often cited as evidence of such unwarranted duplication of costly facilities [45]. Costs of such facilities are subsidized through higher charges for other more widely used services, and are ultimately reflected in the cost of insurance.

Control over bed capacity and specialized facility growth in hospitals is likely to come from strengthening of comprehensive planning agencies. The major function of these organizations has been to review applications for federal grants or loans for construction of health facilities or other capital expenditure. Planning agencies have been largely ineffective because federal funds typically are only a small share of the capital requirements of hospitals. Having other sources of funds, hospitals have been able to ignore the planning agencies. To increase the power of planning agencies, many states have passed legislation requiring that proponents of new facilities obtain a certificate of need. Certificates presumably would be issued only when clear need for the proposed facility is established. The Social Security Amendments of 1972 also strengthened planning agencies by permitting HEW to withhold reimbursement amounts to providers for costs related to capital expenditures that are inconsistent with state or local health plans.

While controls on capital expenditures appear desirable in the light of evidence of market failure, several issues can be raised. How does one "objective-

---

[a]Unlike other studies, we did not find a significant relationship between hospital utilization of Medicaid eligibles and hospital bed availability. The absence of the expected relationship may have been due to (1) reduced importance of the supply-creates-demand phenomenon in hospitals which provide care for a large proportion of the poor, e.g., state and local hospitals, or (2) state review of cases for excessive lengths of stay.

ly" define need? It seems entirely possible that "need" will come to vary with the extent of a budget constraint so that wealthy areas will have higher "need" levels than poor areas, as at present. The introduction of national health insurance, to the extent it results in increasing the demand for inpatient services, will change the perception of "need" as well in many areas. How competent and free from the influence of existing hospitals are planners likely to be? It seems likely that consumer interests will be weak relative to hospital representatives in planning agencies, if only because of unequal access to accurate information, with the possible result that hospitals will gain approval for projects at roughly the present rate. Will construction controls limit the rate of introduction of cost saving innovations? Hospital interests may be able to "use" planning agencies to restrict entry by more efficient producers, as in other regulated industries. While innovations in the hospital industry have largely been quality and cost increasing, limitations on market entry may further weaken whatever competitive forces presently exist.

Utilization Review

Utilization review is currently being proposed as an appropriate technique for controlling excessive or unnecessary use of services and for maintaining quality. The establishment of peer review in the form of Professional Standards Review Organizations (PSROs) has been mandated by the 1972 Social Security Act Amendments. Some 300 or more PSROs would be formed by groups representing substantial numbers of practicing physicians in local areas and would assume responsibility for comprehensive review of services provided under Medicare and Medicaid. Under this arrangement, physicians would not be reimbursed by Medicare or Medicaid for services viewed as excessive by the local PSRO, or for service delivery which is below established minimum quality standards.

The problem addressed by PSROs is extremely complex in that they attempt to insure that every patient receives care which is consistent with established norms. First, there is the awesome task of establishing rigorous standards for a large number of case types, when the care which is appropriate will vary with the patient's age, medical history, and several other factors. Second, there is the difficult problem of finding agreement among physicians on appropriate norms even for similar cases.

PSROs may eventually become an effective method of controlling hospital admissions and length of stay, surgery rates, the prescribing of drugs, and use of laboratory and X-ray facilities. They should be particularly effective in cases where the prescribed care is obviously excessive. One obvious weakness of the approach is that the loyalties of physicians to members of their profession coupled with the threat of malpractice suits may render them reluctant to be sufficiently critical of utilization decisions. However, the threat that the utilization review process will be placed in the hands of federal and state health departments if PSROs fail may be sufficient incentive to insure their success.

The mandate of PSROs is not merely to reduce the amount of excessive, unnecessary services provided, but to increase the quality of care of individuals whose care is inadequate. In the process of developing norms of appropriate care, standards can easily be set at a level which, in a resource allocation sense, are either too high or too low. While standards or norms will be established by physicians, the decisions which have to be made are not merely medical but economic ones. If standards are set too low, the cost of medical care would fall but care which society is willing to financially support would not be permitted. Likewise, the result of excessively high standards would be that resources would be employed in the delivery of health services which would have a greater value to society if used elsewhere.

One might readily argue that while the utilization and quality levels arrived at through peer review would differ from the socially optimal levels observed in a smoothly functioning market, the results obtained would be far better than under the present largely uncontrolled arrangement. But even this pleasant outcome is not entirely assured. It is quite possible that a high proportion of health services presently rendered to Medicare and Medicaid clients will be found to be below established standards. This is especially likely to occur because it is providers who are setting the standards of "appropriate" care. If more care is presently rendered below the standards, at whatever level they are set, than above them, utilization and costs will increase, not fall, as a result of peer review.

Health Maintenance Organizations and Medical Society Foundations

Concern with inefficiency in the health care system has led to considerable interest in two alternative modes of delivery organization: health maintenance organizations and medical society foundations. The basic objective of both delivery modes is to offer comprehensive health services to voluntarily enrolled consumers through annual contracts on a fixed price (capitation) basis. The fixed price is expected to cover the cost of all needed services for some period such as a year. The two modalities differ primarily in their provider organizations.

The health maintenance organization is usually associated with a large-scale multi-specialty provider organization. Unlike traditional forms of medical practice, the HMO has strong incentives to provide consumers with a combination of health services produced in a technically and economically efficient manner. Considerable evidence has accumulated in recent years which supports the argument that HMOs lead to fewer unnecessary hospital admissions, shorter hospital stays, substitution of ambulatory care for in-hospital care and give greater emphasis to preventive care [12]. HMOs might also be more efficient by reaping economies of scale in ambulatory care. Economies of scale are thought to exist in medical practice because of the more efficient use that can be made of specialized facilities and manpower, the savings in procurement of drugs and appliances, the efficiency permitted in record keeping, billing, and other clerical tasks, etc. However, while the existence of economies of scale seems theoretically reasonable, it has not been empirically demonstrated [5, 31]. The organizational form and the incentives generated by the prepayment mechanism also make it more likely that HMOs will make better and more efficient use of various types of specialized (non-physician) personnel. That medical practice can become more efficient through the use of non-physician personnel has been shown by Reinhardt [38] and Smith et al. [44]. Again, it has not been demonstrated that HMOs do, in fact, make more efficient use of non-physician manpower. Other sources of efficiency that have been demonstrated include more rational use of prescription drugs [30], substitution of psychiatric care for general physician services [20], and substitution of extended care and home health services for hospital days [24]. Finally, large multi-specialty group practice may offer considerable savings in patient time by providing a wide range of services in a single location.

While there are considerable advantages to the HMO form of delivery, they are not without their critics. First, HMOs may be less accessible for many of the poor than the traditional provider. Large-scale multi-specialty practice implies a centralized location. This means that transportation to the HMO, for many of the poor, will be more of a burden than the trip to a nearby private practitioner. HMOs can presumably alleviate this problem by providing transportation or setting up satellite clinics, but this increases the cost of operation.

One of the principal problems HMOs have faced in increasing enrollment among the non-poor is an alleged impersonality in care delivery. Donabedian cited numerous patient complaints found in the literature on prepaid group practice.

There is a certain impersonality about the care received, physicians are not interested and rush the patient out of the office, do not give him the opportunity to explain his trouble exactly, and do not tell him enough about his illness; there is the atmosphere of a clinic and of charity medical care; obtaining medical care is inconvenient; one waits too long to see the doctor; it is difficult to get a home visit [12].

It would seem that all of these problems, to the extent they exist in HMOs more than in traditional forms of practice, would also be disturbing to the poor.

Finally, the prepayment aspect of HMOs also provides an incentive for the organization to economize on the number and quality of its services. However, it is argued that this adverse incentive feature would be tempered by two factors. First, low quality care rendered in the short term may greatly increase costs to the organization in the future. But since the poor are far more likely to frequently change place of residence and thus health care providers, HMOs may view investments in high quality care and preventive medicine as wasteful. Thus, HMOs may be less likely to provide high quality care to highly mobile populations than to non-poor stable populations. Second, it is normally assumed that HMOs would compete with one another and with conventional providers, and that consumers would choose among alternative providers on the basis of price, benefits and quality of service. In such a competitive environment, HMOs would necessarily have to maintain quality to attract patients. This argument rests on the assumption that patients are able to make reasonable accurate assessments of service quality. If the poor are less able than others to make accurate judgments on the quality of care, HMOs would be able to provide a lower quality of care to the poor because the risk of losing them as clients is less.

The medical society foundation is characterized by a number of individual health care providers not formally integrated into a larger organization. Individual providers maintain separate practices and are paid for services by the foundation on a fee for service basis. Because the foundation itself is prepaid, it needs to control costs and attempts to do so through extensive use of local audit and peer review. Individual solo practices are maintained intact under the foundation plan, so that costs are unlikely to be reduced through more efficient provider organization (e.g., scale economies, greater use of non-physician personnel). Rather, the economies are expected to be derived from less use of hospital services, and control of unnecessary physician visits, ancillary services and prescription drugs. Because foundations retain the solo practice mode of delivery, they are likely to offer patients greater convenience, which is of particular importance to patients for whom transportation is difficult. Foundations seem especially well suited for delivery of care in rural areas. Finally, while foundations are not likely to be as efficient in delivery of care as HMOs, they have been considerably more popular with physicians and appear to be growing at a much faster rate.

In considering the merits of these alternatives, it is difficult to overemphasize the importance of an environment in which HMOs and foundations compete against one another as well as traditional providers [27,39]. The minimum feasible size of an HMO is likely to be rather large, say 30,000 to 50,000 members. Reinhardt has observed that large enrollments

... are dictated to some extent by the requirement that the HMO pool and bear some of the financial risks of illness formerly borne by its subscribers individually, and that effective risk-minimization through pooling of risks requires a large "portfolio" of subscribers. Furthermore, the typical HMO is likely to be characterized by relatively high annual fixed costs which ought to be spread over as large a population as possible [38].

If the optimal size of an HMO is, in fact, very large, it increases the likelihood that a single HMO or foundation may come to dominate in many localities or that a few organizations may monopolize health care delivery in an area.

Foundations, in fact, seem to be consciously designed to monopolize care in particular regions and appear to have occasionally been developed in response to the threat of entrance in the market of an HMO. If a single or a few HMOs or foundations came to provide all care in a given region, the result could be either high capitation rates or low quality or both. This is likely to be followed by public demands for regulation. But the results of public regulation in other industries does not leave one optimistic about the likely effects in this one.

A final point concerns the attractiveness of HMOs and foundations to the poor under national health insurance. The usual attractive feature of HMOs is a comprehensive package of benefits and lower costs. The poor presently have a broad set of benefits if covered by Medicaid, and would presumably have a comprehensive benefit package at little or no cost under a national health insurance plan. HMOs and foundation plans would have to compete for clients by eliminating whatever cost sharing exists or by offering whatever services are not included in the insurance plan.[b] As a result, HMOs and foundation may have considerable difficulty in attracting the poor particularly if the deductibles and coinsurance faced by the poor are low and the difference in costs between HMOs and other providers is small.

Conclusions

We have examined several policies which may be more effective in controlling health care costs than present arrangements. We discussed several problems that may occur with each of them. It should be again emphasized that little is currently known about the efficacy of any of these policies particularly when adopted on a broad scale. Because of this reality, the chapter has been highly speculative. We would like to re-state two conclusions mentioned in the beginning of this chapter. First, because several problems can occur with any of these policies, considerable care should be taken in their design and implementation. Second, it is critically important that an equitable and easily administered system of deductible and coinsurance provisions be designed and employed as an additional cost control measure.

Note

1. For a comprehensive review of issues in incentive reimbursement, see Reimbursement Incentives for Hospital and Medical Care, (U.S. Dept. of H.E.W. Research Report) and William L. Dowling, "Prospective Reimbursement of Hospitals," mimeograph

[b]HMOs might also compete for clients by offering care of higher quality; but since patients are notoriously poor judges of the quality of health care, this is unlikely to be an effective strategy.

7 Summary and Conclusions

The final chapter will summarize the most important findings and conclusions of the study. First we discuss the principal findings of Chapter 2, which analyzed issues of equity and efficiency and the causes of rapid cost increases throughout the program. We then summarize the results of the empirical investigation of the determinants of utilization rates for hospital inpatient care and physician services in Medicaid which is presented in Chapters 3 and 4. Then we review the problems raised in Chapter 5 with those features in the leading national health insurance plans which would affect the poor. Finally, we summarize our discussion in Chapter 6 of policies which would increase the efficiency of the delivery system.

Lessons of Medicaid

In Chapter 2, we described the role of the states in administration of the program including the determination of eligibility criteria and benefits. We made estimates of the coverage of the poverty populations in each state as well as estimates of the variation in the value of the Medicaid program to eligibles in each state. The chapter also contains a discussion of current methods of reimbursement for physician services, focusing on the lack of efficiency inducing incentives contained in most schemes. In the final section, we analyzed the growth in Medicaid costs from 1967 to 1972.

The main conclusions from our analysis are the following.

1. The Medicaid program has made significant progress in providing protection for the poor against the costs of health care services. Over eighteen million poor persons currently use services under the program. These individuals use services which would otherwise be denied them because of cost or for which they would incur a significant financial burden. Medicaid has caused an increase in the willingness of many hospitals and physicians to provide care to the poor. In addition, Medicaid pays for premiums to enroll the aged in Medicare and pays deductibles and coinsurance for services covered by Medicare for the indigent aged. The program has also financed a major expansion of nursing home care for the aged and chronically ill, with total payments to nursing homes of over $1.3 billion dollars in 1970.

2. While coverage has expanded dramatically during the history of the program, many poor persons are still not covered. Coverage of the poor varies

109

widely by state, so that less than 10 percent of the poor are covered in some states while most of the poor and many of the non-poor are covered in others. Benefits provided those eligible under the program also vary widely by state. Expenditures on services states are required to provide to groups they are required to cover are ten times as large in some states as in others. Expenditures on optional services per eligible person vary far more widely. As a result, individuals in states which provide little support to the program still bear the costs of much of their medical care. There seems to be little economic or social rationale for such broad variation in program coverage. Any meaningful reform of current arrangements would necessarily provide for a much smaller role for the states. Provisions which permit states to determine eligibility and benefits would most likely lead to the same inequities observed in the present Medicaid program.

3. There are insufficient incentives in Medicaid for consumers as well as hospitals, physicians, and other providers to use scarce resources efficiently. Because of the poverty status of the eligible population, no cost sharing is imposed on use of any service. Yet, with few exceptions, no alternative mechanism for monitoring consumer demand has been substituted. At the same time, methods of reimbursing physicians and hospitals place few incentives on these providers to control utilization and costs. Full cost reimbursement for hospitals permits the provision of services for which there is limited economic demand as well as the purchase of equipment and the hiring of personnel as long as a general increase in hospital rates will cover the additional expenditure. The normal market reaction to high prices (increases in supply and decline in demand) is limited by the non-profit status of most hospitals and the inability of consumers to make independent judgments on the appropriateness of service utilization.

Reimbursement of physicians on a usual and customary fee basis also provides weak incentives for efficient use of resources. Once the maximum permitted fees become widely known, there is no reason for physicians to charge covered patients below those levels. As long as fees paid under Medicaid are above the cost of service delivery, output of physicians might increase so that services desired by Medicaid eligibles would be provided. Provision of desired services, however, is not the only result one might expect. Generous reimbursement may also increase physician incomes with little increase in output, or result in expanding the quality and cost of services. Finally, charges above costs of service delivery (including the implicit cost of the physicians' own time) may lead to inefficient use of inputs without affecting service delivery; that is, permit duplication of facilities, excess manpower, and excessive wage and salary scales in physician practices.

4. Medicaid costs have risen, for persons receiving cash assistance, at 24.8 percent per year for the aged, 34.5 percent per year for the disabled, and 36.6 percent per year for AFDC families. Rates of increase of expenditures for the

medically needy were lower but, nonetheless, fairly rapid. Our analysis showed that costs of a program of subsidized care for the poor need not escalate at rates approaching those under the current Medicaid program. The Medicaid experience has largely been due to the growth of public assistance generally, and not merely the predictable outcome of subsidization. The most important reason for increases in Medicaid costs over time has been the increases in the number of people eligible. During the 1967-1972 period, new states continually entered the program and public assistance eligibility criteria were greatly liberalized. The result was an increase in the number of persons receiving public assistance and thereby becoming eligible for Medicaid. Under a continuation of the present Medicaid program, increases in the number of eligibles would be a much less important factor because public assistance caseloads are stabilizing and all but one state is currently participating in Medicaid. A program with broad population coverage would avoid the problem of continually rising costs because, while large measures in eligibility and utilization would occur following the initial expansion of coverage, they would not continue over time.

In Chapters 3 and 4, we presented an empirical investigation of the causes of variation across states in Medicaid expenditures per eligible person for hospital inpatient care, medical services, and hospital outpatient care. Expenditures per eligible person in the highest states are over four times those in the lowest for hospital inpatient care. Variations in expenditures per eligible person are even greater for medical services and hospital outpatient services. We examined the effects of resource availability (hospital beds and physicians), reimbursement arrangements, income, race, and place of residence on utilization of these services. Utilization data for three cash assistance groups, the disabled (APTD), AFDC children, and AFDC adults, were used. The main conclusions from the analysis are described below.

1. Contrary to findings of other studies on the general population, hospital bed availability does not affect use of hospital inpatient services by Medicaid eligibles. This may reflect the impact of the 1967 amendments to the Social Security Act which required that hospitals review admission and discharge decisions on a continual basis. The absence of the expected positive association also suggests that the supply-creates-demand phenomenon may be less prevalent among hospitals which provide care for a large proportion of the poor. Public hospitals tend to provide a large proportion of the care rendered to low income individuals. Occupancy rates in public hospitals are low relative to voluntary hospitals, suggesting that hospital administrators in public hospitals are less concerned with budget deficits, and as a result, make less of an effort to maximize admissions, and extend the length of stay. We also found that hospital bed utilization was lower in states where a high proportion of total beds were in state and local hospitals. This supports the view that public hospitals are less likely to "shift" the demand for services in response to a fall in occupancy rates.

The success the Medicaid program has had in establishing control over hospital bed utilization so that bed supply does not directly determine demand suggests that efforts to gain control for the rest of the population through utilization review, limitations on construction grants, certificate of need legislation, etc., can be effective.

2. The maldistribution of physicians is often mentioned as one of the most serious problems in the health sector. Shortages of physicians lead to difficulties in obtaining appointments, greater travel time, and longer waiting time in doctors' offices. A surplus of physicians, such as seems to exist in several wealthy metropolitan areas, can also result in increases in the demand for services. Patients generally rely heavily on physicians' judgment concerning return visits, lab and X-ray services, prescription drugs, and hospitalization. Thus, the physician as supplier is in the rather unique position of being able to largely control the demand for his services as well as the demand for prescription drugs. (That he cannot completely do so is evident from the number of cancelled appointments, unfilled drug prescriptions, etc.).

We found some evidence that the distribution of physicians affects both the use of inpatient and ambulatory facilities. The results indicate that the availability of physicians affects the percentage of eligibles who used ambulatory services. This supports the view that physician availability would affect utilization by reducing waiting time, delays in seeking care and in obtaining appointments, travel time, etc. We found evidence that physician availability affects positively the level of expenditures per user of both hospital and medical services. This tends to support the view that physicians can influence the demand for services through control of hospital admission and discharge decisions and through prescription of various ancillary services, return visits, etc. It does not, of course, support a value judgment in either direction on the necessity for such services.

Thus, it appears that a policy designed to increase the supply of physicians would affect utilization of health services by the poor. Such a policy would increase the use of ambulatory care, most likely the use of hospital outpatient facilities. In addition, it would probably increase the number and quality of services per user of both hospital care and ambulatory services. However, a policy of increasing the supply of physicians, in order to reach the poor through a "filtering down effect" would be quite inefficient relative to a system of incentives or controls designed to redistribute physicians. Because of the physician's ability to influence utilization decisions, an increase in physician supply is likely to significantly increase the use of services among those currently well served. Thus, any given increase in expenditures on physician training may result in relatively little change in the provision of care to those presently underserved.

3. Reimbursement arrangements have strong effects on expenditures per user of hospital and medical services. We examined the impacts of three alternative

schemes—reasonable charges with maximums equal to the 75th percentile of customary and usual fees, reasonable charges with more restrictive maximums, and fee schedules—on the percentage of eligibles who use services and expenditures per user of the service. We found that the reimbursement arrangement has little effect on the percentage of eligibles using at least one service. This essentially reflects the patients' decision to seek care and, therefore, is not affected by reimbursement methods. On the other hand, the use of fee schedules rather than more open-ended reasonable charges had a strong impact on the level of expenditures per user of both hospital and medical services. Our results suggested that fee schedules reduced expenditures on medical services per user (1) by \$68.96 for the disabled, \$13.22 for AFDC children, and \$64.81 for AFDC adults, relative to customary and usual charges with maximum charges at the 75th percentile and (2) by \$35.45 for the disabled, \$9.35 for AFDC children, and \$44.15 for AFDC adults relative to customary and usual charges with lower maximums. Results in the hospital inpatient equations also indicated that fee schedules had marked effects on the level of expenditures per user of hospital inpatient care.

The data did not permit accurate estimates of the effect of reimbursement policy on the quantity of services delivered. That is, we could not determine if reimbursement policy affects both price and quantity or only the former. Our best estimate is that the quantity effect is small. In addition, we could not make any judgments about affects on the quality of care. The net result is that health care financing programs could obtain significant savings in costs under such programs by employing fee schedules. However, such programs would incur some risk of adverse effects on the quality of services rendered their clients. We also found no evidence of greater use of hospital outpatient services in response to low reimbursement rates for medical services.

4. The physician-population ratio is not, in itself, a sufficient measure of availability. States with identical physician-population ratios might be quite different in the dispersion of their populations. In our analysis, we included the percentage of the Medicaid eligible population living in metropolitan areas as a variable to control for distance. We argued that the greater the percentage of the eligible population living in metropolitan areas, the less the distance from and the greater the accessibility of a given stock of physicians. We found that persons living in metropolitan areas did have greater rates of utilization of physician care. Both the percentage of eligibles who used hospital outpatient services and expenditures per user were higher for states with a high percentage of eligibles living in metropolitan areas. There was no observable difference in use of office-based physician services; thus overall use of ambulatory care is influenced by proximity as measured by living in metropolitan areas. Even with price of services equal to zero, and controlling for income, the rural poor appear to use fewer services under Medicaid than the urban poor. This finding weakens the argument that government interferences with the supply side of the market

might not be necessary. This inequality, of course, may not be meaningful, say, if urban residents overuse services or if the differences in utilization are due to differences in tastes or attitudes about medical care.

5. There is also concern that even under a program providing complete financing, the private sector delivery mechanism may not be responsive to needs of particular demographic groups. The largest of such groups which may be denied care despite complete financial coverage would be blacks. It has been argued that differences in utilization will remain because of racial discrimination by providers or because of lack of access to medical care providers who tend to locate in non-white neighborhoods. If so, either civil rights enforcement or special incentives to locate in non-white areas would be necessary.

Our analysis strongly suggests that non-white Medicaid eligibles have less access than their white counterparts to services of physicians in office based settings. There was a statistically significant difference in the use of medical services for all three groups. There was no observable difference in use of physician services in hospital outpatient settings, so that total use of physician services is greater for whites than for non-whites. That is, a differential in use of medical services exists after controlling for income, education, urban or rural residence, etc., that is attributable to race. The elimination of the monetary barrier to use of medical services has apparently not been sufficient to equalize access in most areas, and a more active supply policy (civil rights enforcement, increased training of non-white physicians, incentives to locate in non-white areas, etc.) would appear necessary if this objective were to be achieved.

6. A final policy issue is the relationship between changes in income among the poor and their use of health services. There is interest in the question of whether improvements in income maintenance programs would affect the propensity of the poor to use health services. There is also interest in the issue of whether increases in income in conjunction with a health service financing program such as Medicaid would be sufficient to insure satisfactory access to and availability of health services or whether separate provisions such as neighborhood health centers would be necessary. In short, would reforms in the nation's income maintenance programs reduce or eliminate the need for a public involvement in the supply of health services? Our results indicate that use of physician services by Medicaid eligibles is quite responsive to income. The income elasticities were highest for children and lowest for the disabled, perhaps because many valuable services for children are preventive and thus in some sense optional or discretionary. If income is high, more of these services are used and, vice versa, if income is low, many services for children are postponed or never obtained. For the disabled, greater hardship is associated with failure to use services and thus utilization is less responsive to changes in income.

Income elasticities are difficult to measure adequately. First, our income elasticities may have been overstated because of a correlation between the level of per capita income of the eligible population and the probability that information on eligibility for and availability of services will be provided. If such information and income are highly correlated, then the income elasticities are overstated. However, expenditure per eligible on optional services was used to control for the effects of the attitude and generosity of the state. Thus, we believe the income elasticities basically reflect the responsiveness of the poor to changes in income. Second, there may be cultural differences between Medicaid eligibles in high income and lo income states. We attempted to control for such differences with race, education and urban-rural composition variables. If cultural differences remain, then, income elasticities are overstated and raising incomes in low income states will have less than the estimated effects.

Because of these statistical difficulties, it is not easy to say whether increases in income would be a more efficient policy for increasing utilization than direct provision or an incentive system to expand the supply of services to the poor. However, the income elasticities were markedly higher than the supply variable (physicians per capita) elasticities. In some cases, there was no evidence that increasing the supply of physicians would have any impact whatsoever. In the case in which physician supply had its most significant impact, hospital outpatient services for children, the supply of physicians would have to be increased by 5 percent to have the same impact as a 1 percent increase in income. And while the cost of a 1 percent increase in income can readily be obtained, the cost of providing incentives to obtain a 5 percent increase in the physician-population ratio in a given area is unknown. In conclusion, our preliminary evidence suggests that an increase in the incomes of the poor is likely to be a more efficient policy than incentives to redistribute medical resources or direct service provision, once the price of services to users is eliminated.

Prospects for Reform

In Chapter 5, we examined the effect four national health insurance plans would have as alternatives to Medicaid. We considered those aspects of the Nixon Administration, Kennedy-Griffiths, Kennedy-Mills, and Long-Ribicoff proposals which would affect low income individuals. The discussion examined provisions for population coverage, cost sharing, physician reimbursement, administration, and financing. We were concerned more with discussion of problems facing each of the plans than with providing a ranking in terms of acceptability.

The Administration (CHIP) plan would increase coverage for many poor people. However, the cost sharing provisions for poor families would result in family outlays which were very large in relation to income even for families with average total medical care bills. For example, four-person families with $3,000 incomes and average medical care costs would have outlays equal to 9 percent of income. Deductibles and coinsurance rates are set at levels which are designed to reduce excessive utilization. But they may be so high that many families would purchase private insurance to supplement the national plan. With supplementary policies, high and middle income families could end up facing lower marginal costs at time of service utilization than low income families. As a result, neither the equity nor efficiency objectives of the plan would be met.

We discussed the physician reimbursement scheme and argued that incentives would be created which would lead some physicians to refuse to see the poor and aged patients and for others to render a lower level of quality of care. The CHIP plan would face also difficult administrative problems, principally in the determination of income. Income calculations are necessary for assigning appropriate premiums, deductibles, and coinsurance rates. Incomes for many families vary widely from year to year and within a calendar year. To preserve equity, adjustments of premiums, deductibles, coinsurance, and maximum liability would need to be made with each important income change. Job turnover would also require changes from the employee plan (EHIP) to the assisted plan (AHIP) or vice versa. Such adjustments could be taxing for the administrative machinery, and may create confusion and frustration for those families whose incomes are subject to frequent change.

Finally, the CHIP plan is financed in a manner which might have serious adverse employment effects. First, families premiums, deductibles, and coinsurance rates increase markedly at $5,000. Second, the premiums employers are required to pay are likely to lead to a reduction in demand for less skilled workers and for older or other high risk workers and an increase in demand for temporary or part-time workers for whom premium contributions are not required.

The Kennedy-Griffiths plan seems to be most generous in its treatment of the poor. However, the plan is likely to be plagued by severe administrative problems which could affect the poor more than the non-poor. It imposes no cost sharing on anyone regardless of income. Instead, the plan relies heavily on budget control and capitation reimbursement to contain costs. While capitation reimbursement can have desirable consequences, it is also likely to have adverse effects on the amount and quality of care given the poor. Health maintenance organizations and other groups accepting capitation have incentives to seek as clients individuals whose expected cost of care are less than the capitation rate or to minimize the provision of services to those whose expected cost of care are above the capitation rate. Since poor elderly and disabled individuals as well as low income families with children are relatively high risks, capitation may adversely affect the level of care they receive.

The Kennedy-Griffiths plan would be plagued by awesome administrative problems. A bureaucratic structure would have to determine budget allocations for each region, calculate capitation rates for different population groups, monitor quality of care and, in general, solve several difficult issues. Failure to operate the program administratively in a reasonably efficient manner, which seems inevitable, could lead to supplemental payments by middle and upper income groups in return for preferential treatment. The poor who are unable or unwilling to pay would receive less care.

The Kennedy-Mills plan would provide broad coverage of health services for all families and individuals who contribute. Unfortunately, those who are unemployed or out of the labor force and not eligible for an income transfer program would not be covered. The plan has cost sharing provisions which are limited to a $1 charge for each drug prescription. There are two problems with the nearly complete exclusion of cost sharing provisions in a plan. First, there is no incentive for low income families to be conscious of the cost of services which would perhaps result in over-utilization and higher program costs. Programs of potentially greater value to the poor may not be funded because of provision of first-dollar medical care coverage to the poor. Second, if cost sharing provisions are completely excluded for the poor, severe "notch" effects occur when they are introduced for the non-poor. Under the Kennedy-Mills plan, costs rise precipitously when cost sharing is introduced for families with income above $4,800.

The Kennedy-Mills plan contains reimbursement arrangements, as in the administration proposal, which could easily lead to two classes of patients because physicians have clear incentives to provide preferential treatment to those able and willing to pay supplements to the required cost sharing. While income related cost sharing features are present, as in the CHIP plan, administrative problems of income determination are not as critical. Payroll taxes increase automatically with income and the cost sharing status of a family changes with only one income change. The Kennedy-Mills proposal also calls for a unified program for the whole population; thus changes from one component of the plan to another will not occur.

The Long-Ribicoff plan provides for comprehensive coverage of low income people. However, it provides for no cost sharing for families below certain income levels ($4,800 for a family of four), thereby providing few incentives for efficient use of services on the part of low income individuals. In addition, cost sharing increases rapidly at income levels above $4,800. The proposal includes a spend-down provision, as in the Medicaid program, whereby a family is eligible for coverage once its annual income minus its total medical expenses are less than the income levels stated above. The spend-down provision is difficult to administer because of problems of income determination. It is also extremely confusing to families above the designated cutoff levels. It is believed that many families under the present Medicaid program fail to understand the program or cannot make precise calculations of their income and, as a result, do not make use of their eligibility for Medicaid coverage. Similar difficulties would face implementation of the Long-Ribicoff plan. The proposal also makes no effort through reimbursement policy to control costs of its plan for coverage of low income families.

In Chapter 6, we discussed alternative public policies for controlling health care costs. The net effect of any national health insurance program would most likely be a significant increase in demand for hospital, medical and other services. Unfortunately, the goal of increasing the access of the poor to health services of satisfactory quality conflicts with the objective of controlling inflationary pressures in the health sector. We argued that reform of the present program for financing of care for the poor will greatly intensify the need for measures to increase the efficiency of the delivery system.

Costs of programs which finance health services might be controlled by alternative methods of reimbursing hospitals and physicians, regional health planning, utilization review, and delivery of care through health maintenance organizations or medical society foundations. Unfortunately, each of these alternatives is fraught with difficulties. Reimbursement of hospitals on a capitation basis is difficult administratively and may adversely affect the quality of care, particularly for the poor and others less able to make judgments about the appropriateness of care. Incentive reimbursement schemes are attractive but effects are difficult to predict. Reimbursement incentives may result in case-mix changes and quality deterioration in high cost hospitals and increased expenditures on capital equipment and professional manpower in low cost hospitals. Difficult decisions of appropriate rates of increase in reimbursement rates as new technology is introduced and input prices rise would still be required.

Fee schedules appear to be effective in controlling program expenditures but may adversely affect the number and quality of services provided. When fee schedules are used for the poor while a less restrictive reimbursement method is used for the rest of the population, incentives are created which are likely to alter physicians' preferences in favor of the latter. The quantity and quality of services rendered to the poor relative to need are likely to be less than that provided the non-poor.

Area-wide health planning may control costs by limiting capacity expansion in institutions, but success depends on the ability of agencies to accurately forecast "need" and to remain free of influence of existing hospitals. Planning may also weaken whatever cost-limiting effects competition may currently be having. Utilization review may limit costs but is likely to prove awkward administratively. Its success in controlling utilization and costs depends largely on the ability of its proponents to establish standards of "appropriate" care which will not be so high that valuable non-medical uses of scarce funds are foregone to finance care at those standards.

Health maintenance organizations and medical society foundations may be successful in providing health services at lower costs than traditional forms of delivery. However, both forms of delivery also have clear incentives to reduce the quality of care, particularly to low income groups. Health maintenance organizations will often be less accessible for the poor than solo or small-group practitioners. HMOs may also have difficulty attracting the poor, particularly under plans where the deductibles and coinsurance faced by the poor are low. Finally, the effectiveness of HMOs in controlling costs and maintaining quality depends to a great extent on the presence of a competitive environment. If such an environment is absent, the result could be higher capitation rates or lower quality or both.

Concluding Remarks

Because much of this study has been critical of Medicaid, it should again be stated that Medicaid has been a drastic improvement on previous arrangements. Undoubtedly, the tone of much of the analysis would have been different if this had been a before-and-after study of Medicaid. It should also be emphasized that while some individuals will be worse off each of the proposed alternatives should improve the system of financing care for the poor. It is hoped that the reforms in financing of care for the poor which are eventually included in a national health insurance plan will be able to solve many of the problems raised in this study. Hopefully, some of the findings contained in this study will be useful to those considering the necessary reforms.

Appendixes

Appendix A
Data Sources

This appendix will discuss sources of data for the work described in Chapters 3 and 4.

Expenditures-Recipients

Data on expenditures and recipients (users) for all services, for all aid categories and for all states was provided by the National Center for Social Statistics (NCSS). States are required by law to report annual totals for expenditures and recipients. Summary statistics are then published in *Numbers of Recipients and Amounts of Payments Under Medicaid and Other Medical Programs Financed From Public Assistance Funds.* The published figures do not distinguish between recipients for whom money payments were authorized and those for whom they were not authorized. The first category consists of those who were receiving cash assistance. The second category includes the medically needy as well as those who are eligible for cash assistance but refuse it and those who are in institutions, such as homes for disabled, aged, etc. Institutions will provide food, shelter and other services. Thus, the maximum income one can have and remain eligible for cash assistance is far lower than for those not institutionalized. The data presented below are limited to the cash assistance population because (1) there is significant variation in state provisions for the medically needy and (2) the available demographic and economic characteristics are available solely for the cash assistance populations.

Only the following thirty-eight states were used in 1969:

1.	California	14.	Maine	27.	Oregon
2.	Colorado	15.	Michigan	28.	Pennsylvania
3.	Connecticut	16.	Minnesota	29.	Rhode Island
4.	Delaware	17.	Missouri	30.	South Carolina
5.	District of	18.	Montana	31.	South Dakota
	Columbia	19.	Nebraska	32.	Texas
6.	Georgia	20.	Nevada	33.	Utah
7.	Hawaii	21.	New Hampshire	34.	Vermont
8.	Idaho	22.	New Mexico	35.	Washington
9.	Illinois	23.	New York	36.	West Virginia
10.	Iowa	24.	North Dakota	37.	Wisconsin
11.	Kansas	25.	Ohio	38.	Wyoming
12.	Kentucky	26.	Oklahoma		
13.	Louisiana				

In 1970, Arkansas, Florida, Indiana, Maryland, Mississippi, New Jersey, Tennessee, and Virginia were added to the data base. Several states which had Medicaid programs were excluded. In 1969, Tennessee did not report the required data. Massachusetts was excluded in both years because the data were estimated from a sample which did not include Boston. Virginia was excluded in 1969 because the data covered only six months. Maryland was excluded in 1969 because the data did not include January. The data reported by California in 1969 contained several inconsistencies and were excluded. However, data from the California paid claims tapes for 1969 were substituted.

Data was also occasionally missing for some states either because the state did not have a program (Nevada has no cash assistance program for the disabled, several states did not cover prescription drugs) or because data were not reported. Specific states were excluded from certain regressions in cases where data appeared to be grossly in error in order to eliminate possible bias in the parameter estimates.

Eligibles

We made estimates of eligibles because of an expectation of variation in ratios of recipients to eligibles across states. NCSS does not have estimates of eligibles, nor is it clear how eligibility should be defined. Use of all persons below the poverty index would exclude all persons receiving cash assistance who are above the poverty line and include many below the line who would not be categorically eligible. Use of the unduplicated count of all recipients of one or more services would exclude all who used no services, which most likely varies widely across states. Our decision was to include as eligibles all those who were recipients of cash assistance at any time during the year. This would include as eligibles even those receiving assistance for one or two months. They are considered eligible for Medicaid because any significant health problem while not eligible would probably result in reapplication for cash assistance and Medicaid coverage. This is obviously an imprecise measure of program eligibles but is the best that could be developed. A turnover variable (see below) was introduced to control for variation across states in short-term eligibility.

Estimates of eligibles for disabled, AFDC adults, and AFDC children were made in the following manner. We began by taking the cash assistance caseloads for each state for December 1968 (1969) and adding all cases approved for cash payments during 1969 (1970). The 1968 (1969) closing caseloads were taken from the *Advance Release of Statistics on Public Assistance Including Medicaid: December 1968* (1969). The data on case openings were estimated from publications of *Applications, Cases Approved and Cases Discontinued for Public Assistance*. For 1970, these data permitted us to make estimates of maximum Medicaid eligibles, that is, actual caseload (12/69) plus all 1969 openings.

However, this publication was not available for the first two quarters of 1969. Estimates for these quarters were made on the basis of the final two 1969 quarters and four quarters of 1970. Thus, total 1969 openings was equal to:

$$\sum_i^4 A_i = (A_3 + A_4) \left(\frac{A_5 + A_6}{A_7 + A_8} \right) + A_3 + A_4$$

where

A_i = cases approved in quarter i,

i = 1 in first quarter 1969;

i = 2 in second quarter; etc.,

and total closings were equal to

$$\sum_i^4 C_i = (C_3 + C_4) \left(\frac{C_5 + C_6}{C_7 + C_8} \right) + C_3 + C_4$$

where

C_i = cases discontinued in quarter i,

i = 1 in first quarter 1969;

i = 2 in second quarter 1969; etc.

Actual end of year 1969 caseloads were available from Public Assistance Statistics: December 1969. Taking the end of year 1968 caseload estimates and adding our estimated openings and closing did not yield numbers exactly equal to the actual 1969 caseloads. Therefore, the following adjustments were made to improve the estimates of openings and closings:

A. If the actual caseload (12/69) $>$ estimated caseload (actual caseload $-$ 12/68 + $\sum_i^4 A_i$), we

1. added ½ of difference to openings
2. subtracted ½ of difference from closings

B. If the actual caseload (12/69) < estimated caseload (actual caseload −

$12/68 + \sum_{i}^{4} A_i$), we

1. subtracted ½ of difference from openings
2. added ½ of difference to closings.

This gave us a series of adjusted openings. Thus our adjusted maximum cases, or maximum Medicaid eligibles was constructed from actual caseload (12/68) plus adjusted openings for 1969.

Turnover Rates

An index of turnover was developed to use as a control variable because of variation in short-term eligibility among states. Turnover is not easily defined or measured. We used a definition suggested by NCSS which called for dividing adjusted 1969 (1970) closings (as defined above) by the 12/68 (12/69) caseload plus adjusted 1969 (1970) openings (also defined above). This gives a measure of the total number of cases discontinued over total cases. This estimate is biased to the extent there is significant re-opening of cases. However, case re-openings have been estimated at only 1.8 percent for the nation [43]. Thus, any biases should be minor.

Demographic and Economic Characteristics
(APTD)

The data sources for the demographic and economic characteristics of APTD recipients—median age, percentage female, percentage living with spouse, percentage non-white, percentage residing in SMSAs, percentage high school graduates—are published in *Findings of the 1970 APTD Study, Part I: Demographic and Economic Characteristics* and *Part II: Financial Characteristics*, both published by the National Center for Social Statistics in HEW—SRS.

Demographic and Economic Characteristics
(AFDC)

The data sources for the demographic and economic characteristics of AFDC were the *Findings of the 1967 AFDC Study, Part I: Demographic and Program Characteristics* and *Part II: Financial Characteristics*, and *Findings of the 1969*

AFDC Study, Part I: Demographic and Program Characteristics and *Part II: Financial Characteristics*. The 1967 survey was a 3 percent sample of AFDC cases and provided data for all regions and all states. The 1969 survey was a 1 percent sample and provided data for all regions but only selected states. We used both data sources to make estimates of age, percentage non-white, education, percentage in SMSAs, average total income, and average earned income. For example, the percentage of the eligible population which was non-white was estimated for 1969 using data from 1967 and 1969 in the following way.

$$\left(\frac{NW}{TOT}\right)_{ik}^{69} = \left(\frac{NW}{TOT}\right)_{ik}^{67} \left\{ 1 + \left[\frac{NW_k^{69} - NW_{jk}^{69}}{TOT_k^{69} - TOT_{jk}^{69}} - \frac{NW_k^{67}}{TOT_k^{67} - TOT_{jk}^{67}} \right] \right\}$$

where

$\left(\dfrac{NW}{TOT}\right)_{ik}^{69}$ = proportion of AFDC population non-white in state i in region k in 1969.

$\left(\dfrac{NW}{TOT}\right)_{ik}^{67}$ = proportion of AFDC population non-white in state i in region k in 1967; i includes only states for which data are not reported in 1969.

NW_k^{69} = the non-white AFDC population in region k in 1969.

NW_k^{67} = the non-white AFDC population in region k in 1967.

TOT_k^{69} = the total AFDC population in region k in 1969.

TOT_k^{67} = the total AFDC population in region k in 1967.

NW_{jk} = the non-white population in state j in region k where j states are those for which data were reported in 1967 and 1969.

TOT_{jk} = the total population in state j in region k where j states are those for which data were reported in 1967 and 1969.

The 1970 demographic and economic characteristic variables were created by adding one-half of the difference between the 1969 and 1967 values of the variable to the 1969 variable.

Prices

Hospital Prices

Data on hospital prices were taken from *Hospitals*, American Hospital Association, Vol. 44, No. 15 (August 1, 1970) and from Vol. 45, No. 15 (August 1,

1971). Both revenue per inpatient day and revenue per outpatient visit were derived from this source. The data are for non-federal, short-term general and other special hospitals (non-governmental non-profit, non-governmental for profit, and state and local governmental) other than psychiatric and tuberculosis.

Physician Prices

The only available data on physician prices, by state, is from *Medicare and Medicaid: Problems, Issues, and Alternatives*, a U.S. Senate Committee on Finance report. The publication provides data on average charges for all services and for medical care, surgery, X-ray, laboratory, consultation, anesthesia, and assisting at surgery. The charges are for services rendered to Medicare patients by physicians in each state. A small percentage of these charges were reduced by the fiscal intermediaries. We use average total because it excludes the effectiveness of the intermediary as a variable in determining prices. It should be remembered that these data are imprecise measures of physician charges or fees. Each type of service includes a wide variety of specific procedures, from the very complex and expensive to the simple and inexpensive. The average total charge for all services or for the selected types of services is determined by the level of charges for each service weighted by the frequency with which they are represented in the data. Thus, prices may differ across states because of greater frequency of more costly procedures even if the charge for identical procedures is equal. Prices were adjusted to 1969 and 1970 levels by use of the medical care component of the consumer price index.

Availability

Data on hospital bed-population ratios, doctor-population ratios, extended care bed-population ratios, etc., were taken from various sources.

Population

State population figures were taken from the *Statistical Abstract of the United States, 1971*, published by the U.S. Department of Commerce, Bureau of Census.

Hospital Beds

Data on beds in short-term general hospitals were obtained from *Hospitals*, American Hospital Association, Vol. 44, No. 15 (August 1, 1970) and Vol. 45, No. 15 (August 1, 1971).

ECF Beds

Data on beds in extended care facilities were obtained from *Medicare: Fiscal Years 1968-71, Selected State Data*, DHEW-SSA.

Physicians

Data on total physicians, office-based physicians, hospital-based physicians, primary care physicians (general practice, internal medicine, pediatrics and obstetrics and gynecology), and surgical specialists were obtained from the *Distribution of Physicians, Hospitals and Hospital Beds in the U.S., 1969*, American Medical Association, Vol. 1, 1970, and *Distribution of Physicians in the United States, 1970*.

Appendix B
Users per Eligible and Expenditures per User for Selected Services for All States

Appendix B provides the dependent variables used in the regressions. Data are occasionally missing for reasons given in Appendix A.

Table B-1
Hospital Inpatient Services (1969)

	USERS			EXPENDITURES		
	Disabled	Children	Adults	Disabled	Children	Adults
California	*	*	*	*	*	*
Colorado	.20	.05	.15	679.04	306.11	391.92
Connecticut	.22	.20	.20	1728.39	390.13	659.24
Delaware	.16	.05	.15	886.55	404.22	514.33
District of Columbia	*	.05	.15	*	740.85	735.12
Georgia	.22	.04	.16	786.59	292.75	432.79
Hawaii	.17	.07	.21	987.56	378.63	505.45
Idaho	.19	.06	*	706.93	268.54	*
Illinois	.28	.09	.23	1475.32	511.47	776.68
Iowa	.33	*	*	654.66	*	*
Kansas	.22	.07	.26	1299.14	383.84	630.90
Kentucky	.20	.06	.16	664.83	262.75	400.98
Louisiana	.13	.04	.15	504.93	285.30	287.64
Maine	.27	.09	.22	1271.82	267.37	504.82
Michigan	.22	.08	.25	1299.10	390.15	747.20
Minnesota	.20	.07	.13	1631.48	1110.37	1214.48
Missouri	.18	.06	.19	878.78	253.42	379.75
Montana	.27	.09	.24	582.16	252.75	378.86
Nebraska	.24	.05	.23	1052.33	427.81	427.98
Nevada	*	.09	.26	*	275.72	612.12
New Hampshire	.31	.07	.20	1042.87	289.95	484.98
New Mexico	.19	.06	.20	756.70	293.31	379.98
New York	.15	.07	.15	2344.18	506.97	1073.01
North Dakota	.27	.10	.26	762.93	310.03	388.52
Ohio	.23	.06	.19	1505.27	519.03	670.31
Oklahoma	.23	.07	.09	497.74	316.57	606.35
Oregon	.18	.03	.10	594.59	294.36	401.57
Pennsylvania	.17	.09	.14	936.05	310.82	512.70
Rhode Island	.19	.09	.19	1417.77	454.58	633.56

Table B-1 (cont.)

	USERS			EXPENDITURES		
	Disabled	Children	Adults	Disabled	Children	Adults
South Carolina	.20	.02	.13	373.99	298.20	334.82
South Dakota	.31	.07	.18	797.82	297.50	431.55
Texas	.22	.05	.16	893.51	345.24	533.64
Utah	.23	.11	*	609.29	126.69	*
Vermont	.27	.06	.21	1257.69	378.41	583.94
Washington	.30	.04	.11	567.31	351.10	622.46
West Virginia	.17	.07	.16	695.49	314.80	376.70
Wisconsin	.20	.09	.26	1127.75	334.90	502.07
Wyoming	.21	.09	.20	516.94	230.88	286.52

Table B-2
Hospital Inpatient Services (1970)

	USERS			EXPENDITURES		
	Disabled	Children	Adults	Disabled	Children	Adults
California	.28	.06	.19	1627.21	468.71	603.99
Colorado	.28	.06	.22	741.46	297.04	386.96
Connecticut	.21	.11	.18	1942.88	459.47	758.69
Delaware	.17	.05	.17	1324.26	432.72	577.07
District of Columbia	.13	.06	.20	2264.93	858.28	784.57
Georgia	.23	.05	.20	918.20	326.47	487.92
Hawaii	.23	.07	.20	987.95	378.10	505.12
Idaho	.22	.06	.22	923.75	285.72	495.31
Illinois	.23	.09	.19	1599.11	677.91	822.19
Iowa	.24	.08	.20	661.20	280.85	440.73
Kansas	.25	.07	.22	1305.32	414.79	667.08
Kentucky	.23	.06	.18	821.96	302.45	466.90
Louisiana	.16	.04	.16	666.70	365.90	342.35
Maine	.30	.11	.21	1254.34	300.27	524.50
Michigan	.26	.06	.19	1439.61	495.75	684.61
Minnesota	.27	.09	.21	1444.13	460.10	740.77
Missouri	.18	.06	.16	849.31	276.54	397.41
Montana	.27	.09	.23	624.17	278.86	423.41

Table B-2 (cont.)

	USERS			EXPENDITURES		
	Disabled	Children	Adults	Disabled	Children	Adults
Nebraska	.24	.07	.22	1138.33	462.83	500.85
Nevada	*	.08	.24	*	330.72	632.84
New Hampshire	*	.07	.24	1290.17	312.07	493.08
New Mexico	.20	.06	.16	878.45	290.94	497.07
New York	.14	.02	.21	2282.64	502.61	998.24
North Dakota	.22	.06	.15	885.78	348.09	465.65
Ohio	.23	.06	.17	1617.83	576.91	294.06
Oklahoma	.08	.20	550.04	304.91	294.06	.22
Oregon	.22	*	*	778.72	*	*
Pennsylvania	*	.13	*	1003.63	344.13	*
Rhode Island	.23	.09	.22	1867.27	480.20	615.42
South Carolina	.20	.04	.16	721.14	304.95	470.39
South Dakota	.28	.08	.18	901.39	337.87	490.09
Texas	*	.07	*	881.53	388.63	602.48
Utah	.32	.06	.18	619.16	242.18	335.08
Vermont	.22	.12	.16	1007.75	633.00	664.90
Washington	.18	.04	.12	1117.66	414.40	517.14
West Virginia	.17	.06	.13	739.53	320.05	398.40
Wisconsin	.33	.07	.26	977.02	448.34	647.32
Wyoming	.25	.08	.20	659.37	190.64	332.10
Arkansas	.15	.03	.09	531.45	279.73	354.05
Florida	.18	.03	.13	908.06	454.02	467.99
Indiana	.18	.04	.13	1357.18	363.78	607.66
Maryland	.17	.05	.16	1568.75	646.47	774.15
Mississippi	.15	.02	*	522.84	237.16	*
New Jersey	.16	.05	.09	1319.52	502.21	463.27
Tennessee	.17	.05	.13	579.37	275.71	364.98
Virginia	.22	.06	.18	1130.35	376.86	475.24

Table B-3
Medical Services (1969)

	USERS			EXPENDITURES		
	Disabled	Children	Adults	Disabled	Children	Adults
California	.66	.50	.62	273.56	74.25	165.15
Colorado	.66	.30	.48	95.60	33.72	76.11
Connecticut	.63	.54	.62	135.15	35.65	95.67
Delaware	.60	.54	.62	111.52	27.10	88.80
District of Columbia	*	.11	.28	*	57.85	84.38
Georgia	.54	.27	.45	137.34	36.22	95.09
Hawaii	.70	.76	.62	56.07	15.17	50.35
Idaho	.53	.42	.52	148.57	45.62	122.34
Illinois	.63	.49	.63	72.93	22.00	65.36
Iowa	.79	.56	.43	142.31	44.85	155.02
Kansas	.77	.52	.75	159.78	51.02	146.28
Kentucky	.68	.57	*	90.84	37.91	*
Louisiana	.42	*	.20	77.59	*	105.70
Maine	.62	.42	.60	161.26	40.55	103.57
Michigan	.67	.49	.71	171.94	47.36	138.46
Minnesota	.66	.35	.55	165.38	114.28	165.87
Missouri	.50	.39	.55	122.57	37.80	98.42
Montana	.61	.42	.58	179.22	47.60	125.84
Nebraska	.60	.23	*	149.09	66.84	*
Nevada	*	.44	.66	*	48.82	150.46
New Hampshire	.67	.44	.56	189.34	44.02	118.84
New Mexico	.71	.46	.67	93.77	31.26	72.66
New York	.39	.50	.42	101.45	45.11	70.58
North Dakota	.72	.49	.62	126.65	40.34	107.06
Ohio	.57	.34	.51	85.77	26.87	60.88
Oklahoma	.72	.43	.26	104.94	42.42	181.95
Oregon	.54	.27	.38	80.20	24.53	49.22
Pennsylvania	.68	.61	.64	48.60	18.07	31.22
Rhode Island	.63	.48	.65	77.66	32.80	64.72
South Carolina	.47	.14	.69	107.64	32.83	74.17
South Dakota	.61	.30	.44	171.26	44.47	107.85
Texas	.49	.34	.47	245.70	52.68	143.00
Utah	.41	.20	.44	62.81	34.11	48.88
Vermont	.68	.48	.60	167.34	41.50	106.95
Washington	.47	.32	.52	120.50	29.75	54.82
West Virginia	.84	.51	.78	57.10	31.68	54.24
Wisconsin	.63	.60	.74	130.55	43.79	101.11
Wyoming	.55	.44	.57	109.67	34.55	11.23

Table B-4
Medical Services (1970)

	USERS			EXPENDITURES		
	Disabled	Children	Adults	Disabled	Children	Adults
California	.89	.50	.73	194.08	65.45	140.97
Colorado	.72	.37	.56	117.96	38.04	95.06
Connecticut	.62	.49	.57	112.10	33.93	78.87
Delaware	.68	.56	.61	117.15	29.81	93.08
District of Columbia	.18	.19	.44	140.76	52.10	128.46
Georgia	.67	.36	.58	*	47.02	132.78
Hawaii	*	.57	.52	104.94	43.64	106.08
Idaho	.58	.39	.57	168.68	47.52	136.69
Illinois	.65	.47	.56	114.60	39.37	101.04
Iowa	.78	.54	.67	122.56	44.84	107.43
Kansas	.81	.46	.64	142.16	48.88	135.95
Kentucky	.66	.51	.71	79.88	31.43	60.43
Louisiana	.35	*	*	71.30	*	100.80
Maine	.81	.50	.67	128.51	39.58	81.10
Michigan	.69	.38	.51	166.70	46.40	128.01
Minnesota	.72	.60	.73	175.87	52.73	117.89
Missouri	.48	.34	.47	119.08	36.38	93.46
Montana	.60	.39	.56	173.20	49.70	132.74
Nebraska	.61	.36	.51	153.61	48.70	122.75
Nevada	*	.37	*	*	48.21	*
New Hampshire	.73	.43	.61	117.51	37.60	95.23
New Mexico	.67	.37	.53	110.85	36.03	93.30
New York	.51	.51	.67	93.54	32.24	66.60
North Dakota	.58	.28	.40	147.68	55.10	124.33
Ohio	.58	.28	.44	80.42	26.85	56.94
Oklahoma	.63	*	.75	112.25	35.10	59.83
Oregon	.65	.18	.29	81.91	35.98	81.94
Pennsylvania	.71	*	.80	52.51	*	33.95
Rhode Island	.70	.49	*	94.43	36.74	55.06
South Carolina	.60	.33	.53	119.55	30.85	91.62
South Dakota	.58	.32	.44	154.36	42.71	103.59
Texas	*	*	*	*	*	*
Utah	.45	.13	.26	64.74	46.00	62.95

Table B-4 (cont.)

	USERS			EXPENDITURES		
	Disabled	Children	Adults	Disabled	Children	Adults
Vermont	.71	.56	.62	121.68	66.28	74.56
Washington	.61	.32	.42	102.61	43.52	81.09
West Virginia	*	.42	.61	57.41	33.52	57.86
Wisconsin	.70	.48	.71	*	55.87	152.32
Wyoming	.59	.38	.54	147.39	33.73	83.97
Arkansas	.39	.27	.34	62.68	21.81	46.26
Florida	.29	.12	.24	118.37	38.04	87.16
Indiana	.47	.32	.49	135.74	37.87	102.40
Maryland	.72	.36	.58	50.84	18.24	36.49
Mississippi	.45	.21	*	74.36	24.72	*
New Jersey	.65	.33	.56	102.45	48.52	45.18
Tennessee	.37	.19	.29	*	22.96	48.14
Virginia	.52	.33	.44	135.71	46.44	105.64

Table B-5
Hospital Outpatient Services (1969)

	USERS			EXPENDITURES		
	Disabled	Children	Adults	Disabled	Children	Adults
California	.334	.174	.231	164.80	41.34	63.97
Colorado	.284	.110	.189	64.09	28.04	38.95
Connecticut	.386	.355	.429	85.19	30.46	57.10
Delaware	.380	.313	.393	68.26	26.36	46.44
District of Columbia	.405	.350	.460	59.73	28.50	41.89
Georgia	.236	.111	.204	45.65	17.01	29.86
Hawaii	.407	.255	.332	120.32	48.61	85.94
Idaho	.191	.114	.074	43.60	16.65	76.36
Illinois	.321	.249	.343	121.77	29.95	111.86
Iowa	*	*	*	*	*	*
Kansas	.205	.213	.301	73.91	25.15	38.69
Kentucky	.181	.149	.214	37.41	17.66	26.77
Louisiana	.224	.120	.248	19.23	8.95	14.24
Maine	.290	.193	.325	44.23	18.91	26.00
Michigan	.344	.426	.354	54.24	24.99	38.38
Minnesota	.162	.102	.127	74.12	37.82	59.46
Missouri	.241	.218	.285	69.70	25.25	43.14
Montana	.200	.117	.192	44.02	16.48	29.79
Nebraska	.171	.110	.348	54.40	22.23	28.97
Nevada	*	.125	.240	*	23.50	40.02
New Hampshire	.286	.159	.287	47.21	13.89	22.08
New Mexico	.211	.105	.180	29.26	16.59	18.79
New York	.360	.367	.386	85.38	46.51	46.32
North Dakota	.098	.084	.112	29.01	17.09	30.44
Ohio	.417	.316	.426	71.83	26.70	42.96
Oklahoma	*	*	*	*	*	*
Oregon	.205	.075	.115	31.36	17.45	21.83
Pennsylvania	*	*	*	*	*	*
Rhode Island	.369	.321	.431	77.86	34.25	51.01
South Carolina	.136	.037	.173	30.44	15.84	20.76
South Dakota	.115	.078	.095	54.90	13.73	23.44
Texas	.175	.128	.193	72.57	27.51	48.73
Utah	.423	.194	.460	82.41	36.78	38.24
Vermont	.278	.157	.272	46.48	24.70	31.97
Washington	.201	.101	.165	36.24	20.32	27.14
West Virginia	.215	.140	.214	25.86	17.42	21.20
Wisconsin	.184	.257	.315	60.72	25.50	36.79
Wyoming	.181	.131	.203	39.18	15.61	25.02

Table B-6
Hospital Outpatient Services (1970)

	USERS			EXPENDITURES		
	Disabled	Children	Adults	Disabled	Children	Adults
California	.40	.17	.29	144.31	44.14	63.38
Colorado	.30	.12	.21	72.48	30.29	39.72
Connecticut	.37	.33	.41	102.73	41.67	71.25
Delaware	.42	.28	.35	67.19	26.42	50.41
District of Columbia	.42	.35	.50	104.45	40.63	75.17
Georgia	.31	.17	.30	61.28	21.23	37.25
Hawaii	.37	.17	*	172.33	*	*
Idaho	.22	.12	.25	46.69	19.16	30.32
Illinois	.32	.25	.32	130.30	50.02	78.73
Iowa	.19	.17	.24	60.11	22.68	38.13
Kansas	.22	.19	.27	67.79	26.22	40.50
Kentucky	.21	.16	.24	46.47	19.12	29.08
Louisiana	.21	.12	.23	21.52	10.53	15.75
Maine	.37	.24	.35	65.62	22.29	28.77
Michigan	.34	.18	.23	69.63	29.84	44.79
Minnesota	.26	.17	.21	84.22	31.87	44.70
Missouri	.23	.20	.25	65.22	22.13	40.18
Montana	.21	.12	.18	49.16	18.09	26.14
Nebraska	.19	.19	.23	56.69	24.33	34.20
Nevada	*	.15	*	*	33.42	*
New Hampshire	.37	.17	.33	22.54	17.43	25.73
New Mexico	.22	.09	.17	35.61	18.74	27.38
New York	.47	.40	.56	140.95	62.05	77.69
North Dakota	.09	.06	.09	36.41	19.68	33.28
Ohio	.40	.30	.40	66.26	26.27	42.52
Oklahoma	*	.04	.03	21.89	9.85	12.60
Oregon	.27	.09	.14	34.29	19.43	27.95
Pennsylvania	*	*	*	*	*	*
Rhode Island	.46	.32	.61	98.49	40.42	45.64
South Carolina	.20	.11	.20	39.40	17.61	29.51
South Dakota	.12	.09	.11	*	16.65	28.40
Texas	.19	.13	.18	89.61	31.65	52.52
Utah	*	.98	*	*	44.05	*
Vermont	.31	.20	.21	44.07	32.23	34.29
Washington	.25	.11	.15	59.96	24.43	31.51
West Virginia	.24	.13	.19	26.31	18.50	23.01
Wisconsin	.23	.21	.33	*	31.99	58.18
Wyoming	.19	.12	.18	64.22	15.76	22.72

Table B-6 (cont.)

	USERS			EXPENDITURES		
	Disabled	Children	Adults	Disabled	Children	Adults
Arkansas	*	.02	.02	18.09	16.00	16.89
Florida	.25	.11	.20	45.98	25.50	36.57
Indiana	.20	.14	.22	76.01	22.23	38.17
Maryland	.55	.35	.48	110.71	45.85	75.81
Mississippi	.10	.04	*	26.86	13.75	*
New Jersey	.28	.18	.30	105.20	44.51	40.75
Tennessee	.24	.15	.21	58.44	24.15	38.86
Virginia	.33	.23	.32	103.30	33.21	62.44

Appendix C
Means and Standard
Deviations of Variables in
Regression Analysis

This appendix presents a statistical summary of the data used in each regression. The means and standard deviations for each variable are provided. Means will vary for identical variables in different regressions because of the absence of exclusion of data for particular states. States used in each regression are provided in Appendix B.

Table C-1
Hospital Inpatient Care

	Disabled		Children		Adults	
	Mean	S.D.	Mean	S.D.	Mean	S.D.
USERS	.22	.05	.07	.02	.18	.04
EXPENDITURES	1036.93	445.67	371.30	123.88	534.55	159.90
Docs	11.14	3.42	11.26	3.91	11.40	4.09
Beds	43.41	9.35	43.40	9.61	43.75	9.71
Age	55.07	2.02	25.85	3.50	53.75	7.97
Race	24.77	20.56	42.39	27.27	41.84	26.16
Inc	107.43	22.31	47.17	12.43	47.49	11.82
Ed	12.75	5.81	23.43	9.24	23.44	9.20
SMSA	47.54	27.42	54.85	29.48	55.71	29.56
Turn	22.18	6.97	27.58	10.03	27.73	9.84
Sup	93.10	58.60	11.49	8.82	37.43	23.52
Price	68.10	11.90	69.02	11.56	69.66	12.12

Table C-2
Medical Services

	Disabled		Children		Adults	
	Mean	S.D.	Mean	S.D.	Mean	S.D.
USERS	.61	.13	.40	.13	.54	.13
EXPENDITURES	122.31	43.91	39.98	11.29	93.62	34.25
Docs	8.73	1.92	8.77	1.94	9.01	2.27
Oprim	4.63	.80	4.64	.80	4.73	.91
Age	55.11	2.02	26.05	3.57	54.67	7.29
Inc	108.87	22.91	48.17	11.87	49.05	11.96
Race	24.13	19.84	39.85	26.35	40.84	27.39
SMSA	48.08	27.58	55.33	29.74	57.08	29.74
Ed	13.00	5.93	24.55	9.23	24.80	9.20
Turn	22.15	6.88	28.97	9.74	28.29	10.56
Sup	98.06	62.80	12.40	9.45	38.79	24.02
Price	8.18	1.56	8.21	8.56	8.26	1.57

Table C-3
Hospital Outpatient Care

	Disabled		Children		Adults	
	Mean	S.D.	Mean	S.D.	Mean	S.D.
USERS	.27	.09	.17	.09	.27	.12
EXPENDITURES	66.37	33.59	26.71	11.61	39.38	16.40
HDOCS	2.62	2.03	2.56	1.98	2.66	2.02
Age	55.13	2.00	25.98	3.54	54.19	8.31
Race	24.74	21.33	42.11	27.14	41.07	26.54
Inc	107.61	22.74	47.33	12.25	47.66	12.21
SMSA	47.74	28.01	56.39	29.49	56.67	28.91
Ed	12.83	5.99	23.97	9.59	23.75	9.63
Sup	99.10	62.24	12.24	9.76	38.46	23.91
Turn	22.22	6.73	28.66	9.75	28.07	9.52

Appendix D
Data Sources for Time
Series Analysis

In this appendix, the data sources for Table 2-6 are described. Secondly, the regression equations which are the basis for the table and discussion in Chapter 2, "The Growth in the Costs of Medicaid" are also provided.

Data Sources

Data for Table 2-6 were taken from the following sources:

1. Medicaid Recipients and Payments—U.S. Department of Health, Education and Welfare. National Center for Social Statistics. *Medical Assistance Financed Under Title XIX of the Social Security Act.* Report B-1. February 1967 through December 1972.
2. Eligibles—U.S. Department of Health, Education and Welfare. Social and Rehabilitative Services. *Public Assistance Statistics.* National Center for Social Statistics. February 1967 through December 1972.

   Table 4—Aged   Table 6—Disabled

   Table 5—Blind   Table 7—AFDC

3. CPI—U.S. Department of Labor. Bureau of Labor Statistics. *The Consumer Price Index.* Table I. February 1967 through December 1972.

The recipients and payments data are provided for the middle month of each quarter. The eligible data are available by month so that the middle month of each quarter was used. The data for payments and recipients represent totals for bills paid that month regardless of month of service. It is thus subject to errors which occur because of lags in payments. The most serious consequence is a possible upward bias in the growth rates of expenditures and participation. The estimated growth rates of these variables would in fact be estimates for the rates for an earlier time period. Since the growth rates are declining slightly over time, the rates would be overstated for the period observed. The extent of the bias depends on the average length of the payment lag, which is unknown.

Table D-1
AFDC

Dependent Variable	Constant	Time	Time^2	R^2
Expenditures	1738.97 (626.78)	8.02 (38.00)		.98
Expenditures	1733.31 (411.53)	9.44 (11.19)	−.061 (−1.72)	.98
Eligibles	1511.94 (508.51)	5.54 (24.48)		.96
Eligibles	1506.70 (327.29)	6.85 (8.12)	−.05 (−1.46)	.96
Participation	148.60 (−59.46)	1.54 (8.12)		.75
Participation	155.94 (−45.07)	3.38 (4.88)	−.079 (−2.72)	.81
Prices	473.65 (1532.1)	1.19 (50.69)		.99
Prices	472.63 (1166.7)	1.44 (17.85)	−.011 (−3.24)	.99
Services	−98.00 (−35.79)	−.253 (−1.21)		.02
Services	−90.07 (−23.64)	−2.23 (−2.93)	.086 (2.67)	.25
Expenditures*	1675.51 (306.59)	2.92 (7.03)		.69
Expenditures*	1659.71 (218.04)	6.87 (4.50)	−.171 (−2.66)	.76
Recipients*	1281.12 (161.43)	.950 (1.57)		.06
Recipients*	1252.45 (127.51)	8.11 (4.12)	−.311 (−3.75)	.43
Services*	−079.26 (−14.87)	.782 (1.92)		.10
Services*	−065.37 (−8.51)	−2.69 (−1.74)	.151 (2.32)	.27

*Regression estimates for the medically needy.

Table D-2
APTD

Dependent Variable	Constant	Time	Time^2	R^2
Expenditures	1677.76 (670.67)	7.77 (40.79)		.98
Expenditures	1675.97 (413.72)	8.21 (10.12)	−.019 (−0.56)	.98
Eligibles	1298.59 (685.53)	4.70 (32.64)		.98
Eligibles	1294.89 (447.32)	5.63 (9.71)	−.040 (−1.64)	.98
Participation	−77.10 (−60.71)	1.32 (13.64)		.89
Participation	−76.77 (−37.06)	1.23 (2.97)	.003 (.207)	.89
Prices	473.65 (1532.1)	1.19 (50.69)		.99
Prices	472.63 (1166.7)	1.44 (17.85)	−.011 (−3.24)	.99
Services	−017.38 (−5.78)	.548 (2.39)		.18
Services	−14.78 (−3.05)	−.101 (−0.10)	.028 (.689)	.16
Expenditures*	1633.97 (209.09)	7.03 (11.82)		.86
Expenditures*	1612.52 (145.50)	12.39 (5.58)	−.233 (−2.48)	.89
Recipients*	1101.02 (230.42)	5.12 (14.07)		.90
Recipients*	1084.33 (179.12)	9.29 (7.66)	−.181 (−3.54)	.93
Services*	59.29 (12.66)	.720 (2.01)		.12
Services*	55.55 (7.34)	1.65 (1.09)	−0.40 (−0.63)	.10

*Regression estimates for the medically needy.

Table D-3
OAA

Dependent Variable	Constant	Time	Time^2	R^2
Expenditures	1693.34 (402.59)	5.68 (17.76)		.93
Expenditures	1689.14 (250.02)	6.73 (4.97)	−.045 (−0.79)	.93
Eligibles	1421.01 (555.74)	1.75 (8.99)		.79
Eligibles	1415.21 (371.50)	3.20 (4.19)	−.063 (−1.95)	.81
Participation	−105.33 (−35.50)	2.44 (10.81)		.84
Participation	−103.14 (−21.48)	1.89 (1.97)	.023 (.584)	.84
Prices	473.65 (1532.1)	1.19 (50.69)		.99
Prices	472.63 (1166.7)	1.44 (17.85)	−.011 (−3.24)	.99
Services	−95.99 (−26.08)	.301 (1.07)		.01
Services	−95.55 (−15.90)	.192 (.159)	.004 (.093)	.04
Expenditures*	1797.76 (485.35)	4.45 (15.77)		.92
Expenditures*	1804.16 (313.96)	2.84 (2.47)	.069 (1.43)	.92
Recipients*	1291.12 (360.16)	2.44 (8.94)		.79
Recipients*	1279.74 (266.88)	5.28 (5.50)	−.123 (−3.05)	.85
Services*	−311.28 (−323.22)	−.819 (−11.17)		.85
Services*	−306.98 (−329.85)	−1.89 (−10.15)	.046 (5.93)	.94

*Regression estimates for the medically needy.

Bibliography

Bibliography

1. Allen, Jodie. "Cumulative Tax Rate Model." Urban Institute Working Paper 505-2, February 1972.
2. American Nursing Home Association. *The Nursing Home Fact Book, 1970-71.* Washington, D.C.: ANHA, 1971.
3. Anderson, Ronald. "A Behavioral Model of Families' Use of Health Services." University of Chicago Center for Health Administration Studies, Research Series 25, 1968.
4. Anderson, Ronald and Benham, Lee. "Factors Affecting the Relationship Between Family Income and Medical Care Consumption." In Herbert E. Klarman (ed.), *Empirical Studies in Health Economics.* Baltimore, Md.: John Hopkins Press, 1970.
5. Bailey, Richard M. "Economies of Scale in Medical Practice." *Empirical Studies in Health Economics.* In Herbert E. Klarman (ed.), Baltimore, Md.: John Hopkins Press, 1970.
6. Berki, Sylvester, E. "Hospital Economics." Lexington, Mass.: Lexington Books, 1972.
7. Boland, Barbara. "Participation in the Aid to Families with Dependent Children (AFDC)." Joint Economic Committee Print, (Studies in Public Welfare), Paper No. 12, pp. 139-79.
8. Brittain, John A. "The Incidence of the Social Security Payroll Taxes." *American Economic Review*, March 1971.
9. Bunker, John P. "A Comparison of Operations and Surgeons in the United States and in England and Wales." *New England Journal of Medicine*, 282, 3 (January 1970).
10. Davis, Karen. "National Health Insurance." In Barry M. Bleckman et al., *Setting National Priorities: the 1975 Budget.* Washington, D.C.: The Brookings Institution, 1974.
11. Davis, Karen and Russell, Louise B. "The Substitution of Hospital Outpatient Care for Inpatient Care." *The Review of Economics and Statistics* 54 (May 1972).
12. Donabedian, Avedis. "An Evaluation of Prepaid Group Practice." *Inquiry* 6, 3 (September 1969).
13. Dowling, William L. "Prospective Reimbursement of Hospitals." Mimeograph.
14. Feldstein, M.S. "Econometric Studies of Health Economics." Harvard Discussion Paper, No. 291, April 1973.
15. _____. *Economic Analysis for Health Services Efficiency.* Chicago: Markham Publishing Company, 1968.
16. _____. "Hospital Cost Inflation: A Study of Non-Profit Price Dynamics." *American Economic Review* 61 (December 1971).

149

17. Feldstein, M.S. "New Approach to National Health Insurance." *The Public Interest*, Spring 1971.

18. _____ . "The Rising Price of Physicians Services." *Review of Economics and Statistics* 52, 2 (May 1970): 121-33.

19. Feldstein, Paul J. and Severson, Ruth. "The Demand for Medical Care." Report of the Commission on the Cost of Medical Care, *The American Medical Association*, 1964.

20. Follette, W. and Cummings, D.A. "Psychiatric Services and Medical Utilization in a Prepaid Health Plan Setting." *Medical Care* 5, 1 (January-February 1967).

21. Fuchs, V.R. and Kramer, M.J. "Expenditures for Physicians Services in the United States, 1948-1968." National Bureau of Economic Research. Unpublished paper.

22. Goldberger, Arthur S. *Topics in Regression Analysis*. New York: The MacMillan Company, 1968, Chapter II.

23. Holahan, John, and Schweitzer, S.O. "Medical Care Reimbursement, Physician Availability and Provision of Physician Services Under Medicaid." In J. Bergsman and L. Weiner (eds.), *Urban Problems and Public Policy Choices*. New York: Praeger Publishers, 1974.

24. Hurtado, A.R.; Greenlick, M.R.; McCabe, M.; and Saward, E.G. "The Utilization and Costs of Home Care and Extended Care Facility Services in a Comparative Prepaid Group Practice Program." *Medical Care* 10, 1 (January-February 1972).

25. *Hospitals* (Guide Issue). American Hospital Association, August 1970 and August 1971.

26. Klarman, Herbert E. "Approaches to Moderating the Increase in Medical Care Costs." *Medical Care* 7, 3 (May-June 1969).

27. _____ . "Major Public Initiatives in Health Care." *The Public Interest* 34 (Winter 1974).

28. Lee, M.L. "A Conspicuous Production Theory of Hospital Behavior." *Southern Economic Journal*, July 1971.

29. Marmor, Theodore. "Canadian Experience with National Health Insurance: Implications for the United States." Paper presented at Conference on Canadian National Health Insurance, Sun Valley, Idaho, August 25-30, 1974.

30. McCaffree, K.M. and Newman, H.F. "Prepayment of Drug Costs Under a Group Practice Prepayment Plan." *American Journal of Public Health* 58 (July 1968).

31. Newhouse, J.P. "The Economics of Group Practice." *Journal of Human Resources* 8 (Winter 1973).

32. _____ . "Toward a Theory of Non-Profit Institutions." *American Economic Review* 60 (1970).

33. Pauly, Mark V. *Medical Care at Public Expense*. New York: Praeger Publishers, 1971.

34. Pechman, Joseph A. and Okner, Benjamin A. "Who Bears the Tax Burden." Washington, D.C.: The Brookings Institution, 1974.
35. Phelps, Charles E. and Newhouse, Joseph P. "The Effects of Coinsurance on Demand for Physician Services." Office of Economic Opportunity, 1972.
36. Pollak, William et al. "Federal Long-Term Care Strategy: Options and Analysis." Urban Institute Working Paper 970-04-01, October 1973.
37. Rafferty, J. "A Comment on Incentive Reimbursement." *Medical Care* 9, 6 (November-December 1971).
38. Reinhardt, U.E. "A Production Function for Physician's Services." *Review of Economics and Statistics*, February 1972.
39. _____. "Proposed Changes on the Organization of Health Care Delivery: An Overview and Critique." *Health and Society*. Milbank Memorial Fund's Quarterly, Fall 1973. (Quotation from original unpublished manuscript.)
40. Ro, K.K. and Auster, R. "An Output Approach to Incentive Reimbursement for Hospitals." *Health Services Research* 4 (Fall 1969).
41. Roemer. "Bed Supply and Hospital Utilization: A Natural Experiment." *Hospitals*, 1961.
42. Rosenthal, Gerald. "The Demand for General Hospital Facilities." *American Hospital Association*, Monograph 14, 1964.
43. Schiller, Bradley. *Welfare in Review*, September-October 1970.
44. Smith, K.R.; Miller, M.; and Galladay, F.L. "An Analysis of the Optimal Use of Inputs in the Production of Medical Services." *Journal of Human Resources*, Spring 1972.
45. Spencer, F.C. and Eisemen, B. "The Occasional Open-Heart Surgeon." *Circulation*, February 1965.
46. Turem, Jerry. "The Impact on Current Public Assistance Programs of Adopting a Universal Income Supplement." *Technical Studies*, The President's Commission on Income Maintenance Programs. Washington, D.C.: U.S. Government Printing Office, 1970.
47. U.S. Bureau of the Census. *Census of Population 1970*, General Social and Economic Characteristics, Final Report PC(1)-C1, United States Summary. Washington, D.C.: U.S. Government Printing Office, 1972.
48. U.S. Bureau of the Census. *Current Population* Reports, Series P-60, No. 90, *Money Income in 1972 of Families and Persons in the United States*. Washington, D.C.: U.S. Government Printing Office, 1973.
49. U.S. Department of Health, Education and Welfare, National Center for Social Statistics. *Findings of the 1967 AFDC Study, Part I: Demographic and Program Characteristics*, and *Part II: Financial Characteristics*. Washington, D.C.: U.S. Government Printing Office, 1970.
50. U.S. Department of Health, Education and Welfare, National Center for Social Statistics. *Findings of the 1969 AFDC Study, Part I: Demographic and Program Characteristics*, and *Part II: Financial Characteristics*. Washington, D.C.: U.S. Government Printing Office, 1970.

51. U.S. Department of Health, Education and Welfare, National Center for Social Statistics. *Findings of the 1970 APTD Study, Part I: Demographic and Program Characteristics*, and *Part II: Financial Characteristics*. Washington, D.C.: U.S. Government Printing Office, 1972.

52. U.S. Department of Health, Education and Welfare, National Center for Social Statistics. *Medical Assistance Financed Under Titled XIX of the Social Security Act*, Report B-I. February 1967-December 1972.

53. U.S. Department of Health, Education and Welfare. "Social and Rehabilitation Service." *Medicaid* 3, 1 (November 1972).

54. U.S. Department of Health, Education, and Welfare, Social and Rehabilitation Service, National Center for Social Statistics. *Public Assistance Statistics*, February 1967-December 1972.

55. _____. *Recipients and Payments Under Medicaid and Other Medical Programs Financed From Public Assistance Funds*, Report B-4, 1969-1970.

56. U.S. Department of Health, Education and Welfare, Social Security Administration. *Reimbursement Incentives for Hospital and Medical Care*, Research Report, No. 26, 1968.

57. _____. *Social Security Bulletin* 34, 1 (January 1971).

58. U.S. Department of Labor Bureau of Labor Statistics. *The Consumer Price Index*, February 1967-December 1972.

59. Waldman, S. "Average Increase in Costs—An Incentive Reimbursement Formula for Hospitals." *Reimbursement Incentives for Hospital Care*. Research Report No. 26, U.S. Department of Health, Education and Welfare, Social Security Administration, 1968.

60. Weinberger, Caspar. Hearings Before the Senate Committee on Labor and Public Welfare, 93 Congress, 1st Session, 1973.

61. Wilensky, Gail R. *Utilization of Ambulatory Care*. Urban Institute Working Paper No. 963-3, March 1973.

62. Wirick, Grover and Barlow, Robin. "The Economic and Social Determinants of the Demand for Health Care Services." *The Economics of Health and Medical Care*. Bureau of Health Economics and the Department of Economics, University of Michigan, 1964.

About the Author

John Holahan is a member of the senior research staff at the Urban Institute. He has also served as a research analyst for the Ford Foundation Drug Abuse Project and as a lecturer at Trinity College in Washington, D.C. Mr. Holahan received the A.B. in political science from the University of Notre Dame and the Ph.D. in economics from Georgetown University.